INTERPET
HANDBOOKS

UNDERSTANDING
MARINE
FISH

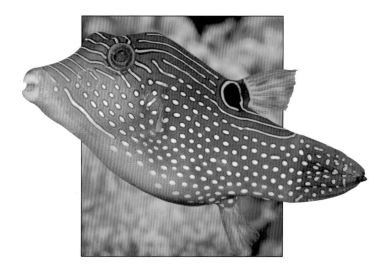

UNDERSTANDING
MARINE
FISH

STEVE HALLS

INTERPET PUBLISHING

© 2001 Interpet Publishing,
Vincent Lane, Dorking, Surrey,
RH4 3YX, England.
All rights reserved.
ISBN: 1-903098-31-9

Credits
Created and designed: Ideas into Print,
New Ash Green, Kent DA3 8JD, UK.
Computer graphics: Phil Holmes and
Stuart Watkinson
Production management: Consortium,
Poslingford, Suffolk CO10 8RA, UK.
Print production: Sino Publishing
House Ltd., Hong Kong.
Printed and bound in Hong Kong.

The author
Steve Halls has been keeping marine
fish for many years and this interest has
extended to his working career. In the
past he has run a marine livestock
distribution company and worked as
sales manager for a major worldwide
marine equipment manufacturer. In his
current role as brand manager for a
major aquatics company in the UK, he
deals with the marine hobby on a
regular basis.

*Below: The forward-facing eyes of the
coral trout* (Cephalopholis miniatus)
enable it to spot its prey from a distance.

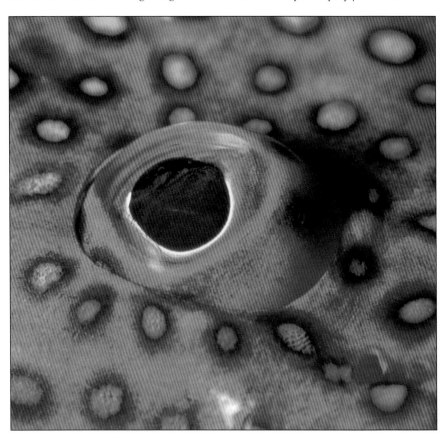

Contents

Note: *Throughout this book, capacities are quoted in litres. To convert litres to imperial gallons, multiply the number by 0.22. To convert litres to US gallons, multiply the number by 0.26.*

Fascinating marine fish

For many fishkeepers, owning and maintaining a successful marine aquarium is the ultimate achievement. There are many reasons for this enthusiasm: the beauty of the natural habitat, the variety of fish shapes and behaviour, the challenge of maintaining the fish in an aquarium environment or just their unrivalled, stunning colours and patterns. It is undoubtedly true that these beautiful creatures have become a fascination for hobbyists throughout the world.

Although the captive breeding of marine fish is increasing, we still know relatively little about how to encourage the majority of marine fishes to reproduce in an aquarium, and to date, most fish offered for sale are still wild-caught. However, the old methods of catching, shipping and keeping marine fish have improved in leaps and bounds, and today's livestock is responsibly caught in hand nets, carefully shipped and well rested and quarantined before being released for sale.

Not only is there a greater understanding of the complexities and requirements of marine fish, but aquarium equipment has also advanced, allowing the fishkeeper to retain far greater control over water quality than used to be the case.

The aim of this book is to combine an understanding of the natural environment of marine fish with the needs of the livestock in an aquarium. The more we can learn about the physiology and natural environment of these stunning fish, the more success we will have in keeping them in our homes.

THE MARINE ENVIRONMENT

With their huge mass, the oceans provide very constant water conditions for their inhabitants. This stability, and the intolerance of many marine species to changes in water conditions, is a key challenge that the fishkeeper must meet.

A large proportion of marine fish inhabit the coral reefs, but the vast size and diversity of the oceans have led to the evolution of many different habitats. These habitats each support species of fish that, in turn, have evolved to suit their surroundings. Some fish are built for speed, some for disguise; some are open-water swimmers, while others inhabit rocky crevices. But despite these differences, they all have one thing in common: they live in saltwater.

The earth's oceans cover more than 70% of the planet's surface.

The fish beneath the waves

A greater understanding of marine fish and the availability of modern equipment have vastly improved the chances of successful fishkeeping.

While the salt content (salinity) varies slightly between the different oceans, their general composition and the ratio of essential trace elements are the same.

Controlling the quality of saltwater in your aquarium plays a vital part in maintaining healthy marine fishes. As very few of us are

The 'salt mix' of natural seawater

Seawater is not simply a solution of sodium chloride; it also contains sulphates, magnesium, calcium, potassium and many trace elements.

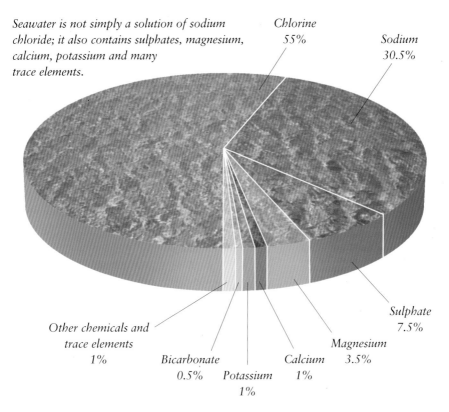

Chlorine
55%

Sodium
30.5%

Sulphate
7.5%

Magnesium 3.5%

Calcium 1%

Potassium
1%

Bicarbonate
0.5%

Other chemicals and
trace elements
1%

fortunate enough to live near clean, tropical beaches, it is important to use a good-quality artificial salt mix, which are now widely available. In reality, most seawater is entirely unsuitable for use in the aquarium, for a number of reasons. Apart from the inconvenience of having to collect it, the inshore waters near human population are often polluted. While fish may survive in this water in the wild, where the supply of water is always being replenished, in the microcosm that is a marine aquarium, natural seawater can be deadly to the aquarium's inhabitants.

Secondly, taking temperate saltwater from local shores and heating it to tropical temperatures is likely to result in bacteria and planktonic blooms. These can cause rapid and severe depletion of oxygen in an aquarium.

Fortunately, a number of high-quality salt mixes are available to the hobbyist, and they are simple to prepare when making regular water changes. The mixes available for the aquarium hobby are very different from table salt. In order for it to support marine life, aquarium salt contains a wide variety of trace elements not present in table salt. Furthermore, salt for human consumption or for domestic appliances has certain additives that make it unsuitable for marine fish.

While many commercially available salt mixes are completely artificial, there is a trend towards using salt mixes with a high level of natural ingredients, thus replicating the composition of natural seawater as closely as possible. Modern production methods, and access to food-grade salt reserves, such as those on the Red Sea, have ensured that the very best salt mixes are indistinguishable from natural seawater.

Salt levels in the aquarium

There are two ways of measuring salt levels in the aquarium, and beginners are sometimes confused by the two phrases used to describe them. The more common unit of

Right: Most hydro-meters are calibrated to operate accurately at 25°C (77°F). If the temperature of your aquarium varies from this, follow the maker's instructions to ensure that you attain an accurate reading.

measurement is 'specific gravity' (S.G.), while outside the hobby it is usual – and more relevant – to discuss salt levels in terms of 'salinity'.

Specific gravity (S.G.)

Specific gravity is the ratio of the density of a liquid compared to that of distilled water. The higher the density and level of minerals and trace elements, the higher the specific gravity. For example, distilled water has a specific gravity of 1, while seawater varies, but is usually found to be about 1.022-1.024.

Salinity

Salinity, meaning the concentration of salts in the water, is quoted in terms of gm/litre or ppt (parts per thousand). The main areas of fish collection for the aquarium hobby are the Red

S.G. and salinity

Specific gravity varies with temperature. When mixing salt, always take the water temperature into account; the warmer the water in the aquarium, the more salt will be required.

15°C	Salinity	25°C
1.022	30 gm/l	1.020
1.023	32 gm/l	1.022
1.025	34 gm/l	1.023
1.027	36 gm/l	1.025

Sea, Caribbean, Sri Lanka, Florida and Philippines. The salinity between these areas varies, but most species will happily adapt to a stable salinity level of about 35 gm/litre (35 ppt) whatever their origin. Salinities vary in nature due to the characteristics of the various oceans. For example, the Red Sea has a high level of evaporation and, therefore, a higher salt content (about 40 gm/litre) than, say, the Pacific Ocean. The extent to which an ocean is tidal will also affect the salinity. The highest salinity is found in the Dead Sea, which is so saline (over 250 gm/litre) that it is impossible for fishes to exist in it.

The key difference between salinity and specific gravity is that the salinity of a body of seawater remains constant, irrespective of temperature fluctuations, while

Above: Green chromis (Chromis caerulea) *in a typical shoal. They live in the Indian and Pacific Oceans, and also in the Red Sea, where the salinity is higher.*

specific gravity readings are temperature-dependent. When keeping aquarium fish, specific gravity is generally measured using a hydrometer. Most hydrometers indicate the temperature to which they have been calibrated (usually about 25°C/77°F) and in general, a change of 10°C (18°F), either up or down, is accompanied by a specific gravity change of 0.001 or 0.0002. As can be seen from the table, cooler water is denser than warmer water.

Various hydrometers are available to the hobbyist, and it is worth paying for the most accurate one you can afford. When measuring specific gravity in an aquarium, be

15

sure to turn off the filters and powerheads, so that you can take an accurate reading. Alternatively, take water from the aquarium and measure the specific gravity in a separate narrow container. This not only provides an accurate reading, but also ensures that the hydrometer does not break on rocks or the side of the aquarium.

It is important to understand that there is no single measurement of specific gravity that is perfect for all marine systems. The key is to provide a stable S.G. and thus avoid stressing the fish. Aim for a reading of between 1.020 and 1.025, and try not to make alterations in specific gravity of more than 0.001 a day.

Commercial systems are often kept at a lower specific gravity than is normally recommended for home aquariums. This is largely due to the resultant lower levels of parasitic and microbial activity. The change in osmotic pressure (see page 23) is tolerated less well by these organisms than by marine fishes. Although this is acceptable for short-term periods, many species will only flourish at higher specific gravity levels.

Fluctuations in specific gravity

Several factors can lead to fluctuations of S.G. in a marine aquarium, and understanding the possible causes will help you to provide a more stable environment.

Left: Shoals of wreckfish (Pseudanthias squamipinnis) *swirl around a coral cliff. These common fish will thrive in tanks if you provide the right water conditions.*

One of the most common mistakes made by new hobbyists when water evaporates from the aquarium is to top it up with freshly mixed saltwater. However, salt does not evaporate, which means that when topping up a tank to counter evaporation, you should only use freshwater. Adding more saltwater will only increase the concentration of salt in the water.

It is not good practice to replenish water in the aquarium only when it has evaporated. Regular water changes are an important aspect of maintaining a healthy aquarium. Bear in mind that when you replace aquarium water with new saltwater, you are also replacing trace elements that are vital to the continued well-being of fish and invertebrates. Replacing 10% of the aquarium water with newly prepared saltwater on a fortnightly basis will help maintain an equal level of salts and trace elements, and contribute to good water quality. If your aquarium has high evaporation levels, be sure to use a hydrometer to test the specific gravity on a regular basis.

Other factors leading to fluctuations in specific gravity include the crystallization of salt on cover glasses and around the tops of protein skimmers and filters. Be sure to keep aquarium equipment free of salt build-up, both for the sake of safety and to maintain a stable level of salt in the aquarium. The protein collected in skimmers (see page 81) will also contain some salt, and this should be allowed for when topping up the tank during a water change.

Tropical and temperate marine fish

The marine fish for sale in aquatic shops are usually tropical varieties, although some specialist shops stock small selections of temperate marines, so what is the difference?

'Tropical waters' clasically describes the areas of the world's oceans between the Tropics of Cancer and Capricorn (23.5° north and south of the equator), but nature has no such rules, and the tropics are thus divided into tropical and subtropical areas. It is from these two areas that the vast majority of aquarium species originate.

At higher latitudes, the sun is less penetrative, so the waters are cooler. The regions where this occurs are known as temperate waters. A vast number of species live in temperate waters, but are often overlooked in favour of their more popular, tropical cousins. However, temperate water fish should not be forgotten as aquarium subjects, as they have a beauty and fascination of their own.

Temperature stability

The large volume of water shared by marine fishes in the oceans is not subject to large temperature swings, although the very upper waters of an enclosed reef or rock pool can be warmed by the sun to a higher degree than open water. It is important to appreciate the stability of temperature that our aquarium fish have been used to in their wild surroundings. A temperature difference of only a few degrees can have adverse effects on many marine species, and should be avoided whenever possible. This is an important issue when considering lighting equipment for marine aquariums; some of the higher-output lighting systems available can generate a great amount of heat. In these cases, it may be worth considering an aquarium chiller to maintain a stable water temperature.

Other important water parameters

As we have seen, marine fishes are accustomed to excellent water quality in their natural habitat and it is vital for every responsible marine fishkeeper to understand the conditions that their fish require. Here we take a brief look at the properties and basic composition of saltwater, as required to maintain a successful aquarium.

Ammonia, nitrite and nitrate

The oceans and reefs from which marine fish originate are generally free from pollutants, such as ammonia, nitrite and nitrate, but all too often these are present in the aquarium. It is imperative to test regularly for these pollutants; coming from 'pure' ocean water, marine fishes are very intolerant of pollution. Fortunately, testing for ammonia, nitrite and nitrate is easy to do, using one of the many test kits available from aquatic centres.

In an aquarium, naturally produced ammonia is broken down into less harmful compounds by bacteria in the filtration system, and by a protein skimmer. If you detect the presence of any ammonia, it is a clear indication that all is not well in

How the nitrogen cycle works

Nitrogen is recycled in the natural world through the digestion of nitrogen-containing proteins by animals and the action of bacteria in the environment. Here is how the cycle works in the marine world.

Fish and other marine creatures digest and metabolize protein as part of their varied diets.

Nitrates are absorbed by plants, such as algae, as a fertilizer.

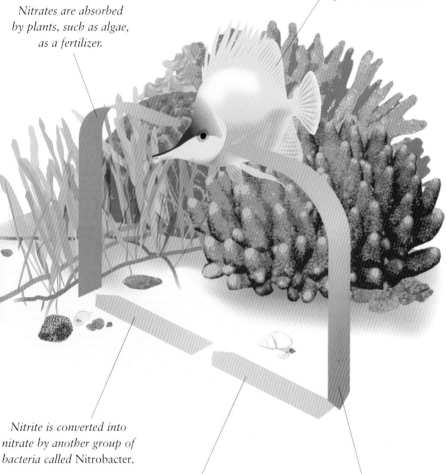

Nitrite is converted into nitrate by another group of bacteria called Nitrobacter.

Ammonia is converted by Nitrosomonas bacteria into nitrite. These bacteria thrive in oxygenated conditions in the substrate and on the surface of rocks.

The main waste product of protein digestion is ammonia. Fish excrete this in urine and directly from the gills. Ammonia also builds up as faeces, plant matter and uneaten food decay.

Water testing

Testing the water involves adding chemicals to a measured sample and comparing the colour change to a printed chart. Some tests, such as this nitrite test, involve adding two chemicals in stages. Allow the correct time period to elapse between adding reagents.

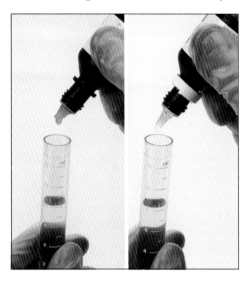

Below: Any indication of the presence of nitrite shows that the bacteria are doing their job, but like ammonia, nitrite is still highly toxic. A zero reading is what you need.

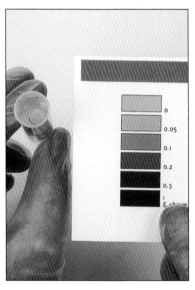

Above: Before using reagents, shake the bottle well. When adding reagents to the sample tube, check how many drops are needed and count them accurately. Make sure that each 'drop' is a complete drop and not half reagent and half air.

the aquarium and immediate remedial action is required. In the short term, this can be done by making substantial water changes and by reducing feeding levels. Continual ammonia readings of anything other than zero indicate either a problem with filtration or overstocking and overfeeding.

Marine fishes are far less tolerant of ammonia and nitrite than freshwater fish, which are often farmed in high stocking densities and have adapted to lower water quality. Even very tiny levels of ammonia or nitrite can quickly kill marine fishes, so regular testing is essential.

pH and alkalinity
Unlike freshwater streams and lakes, where the pH and alkalinity levels vary greatly around the world, the composition of seawater is fairly uniform. A pH level of between 8.0 and 8.4 should be maintained. A falling pH is often an indication that

a water change is overdue, as the alkalinity reserve, or buffering capacity, is depleted.

It is important to test for pH in conjunction with alkalinity reserve, as the pH level of saltwater can drop drastically once the buffering capacity has been depleted. These two tests are an invaluable indicator to the state of the aquarium's water quality and condition. The pH scale is logarithmic, so a pH change from 7 to 8 actually indicates a ten-fold increase. Avoid fluctuations in pH where possible.

Other factors affecting the pH and alkalinity levels in an aquarium can include protein skimming and the uptake of calcium by corals and other organisms in the aquarium. Regular water changes, using a good-quality salt mix, are usually sufficient to maintain a suitable level of alkalinity reserve in the aquarium, although hobbyists with reef tanks may find it necessary to dose regularly with an alkalinity buffer.

Calcium levels
Maintaining a stable calcium level is of more concern if there are invertebrates in the aquarium, as many require calcium to build their skeletons and shells. Low calcium levels will have adverse affects on hard corals and molluscs in particular. However, do not be tempted to maintain artificially high levels of calcium in the aquarium. This will not result in even faster coral growth, but may lead to water quality problems. This is mainly due to calcium's tendency to precipitate out of solution if it is present in excessive quantities. As the calcium precipitates out, it takes essential trace elements with it.

Use an accurate calcium test kit to ensure that levels remain constant at 400-425 ppm (parts per million), and add a calcium supplement if they drop below this range. Performing regular water changes with a good-quality salt mix should provide enough calcium for all but the most heavily stocked reef aquariums.

For those hobbyists struggling to maintain a suitable calcium level, there are several methods of adding calcium to the aquarium (page 93).

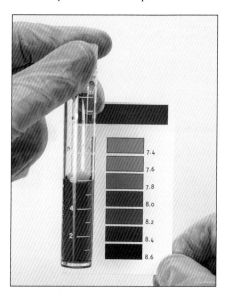

Above: This is the final stage of testing the pH of aquarium water, showing a correct reading of between 8.0 and 8.4. When you compare the sample colour against the printed card, make sure you do it as described in the instructions. Not all tests use the same reading method.

HOW MARINE FISH WORK

Armed with an understanding of how marine fish work, what can harm and distress them, and how best to provide a suitable tank environment, you can avoid making simple mistakes that adversely affect these elegant creatures.

Flattering to deceive

To our eyes this marine betta *(Calloplesiops altivelis)* is stunning, but to potential predators the tail and eyespot mimic a moray eel's head.

Quite simply, saltwater fishes (or marine fishes, as they are more commonly known in the aquarium hobby), are those species that inhabit the oceans and seas around the world. Marine fish include species as varied as the large, predatory – and much-maligned – great white shark, and the small, colourful fish found in abundance swimming in the warm waters around the coral reefs, such as clownfish and damselfish. Many of the fish we consume in vast quantities, such as cod, haddock and mackerel, are also marine fishes, but

they are from cold seas. The fish we are interested in for the purposes of this book are the tropical marine fishes often featured in TV series about life on a coral reef or shown on exotic holiday programmes. They are a varied and intensely beautiful collection of species – the epitome of underwater life on a tropical island.

Keeping marine fishes is now far more affordable and accessible than used to be the case. However, they are challenging fish to maintain and a basic understanding of their needs will make owning a successful aquarium an easier and more enjoyable experience.

The key difference between marine fish and freshwater fish, both coldwater and tropical, is the level of salt found in the water they inhabit, and their ability to survive in their environment. While some freshwater fish may adapt to life in saltwater, and some marine fish will survive at low salinity levels, their inability to cope with the level of salts both in their body and in the surrounding water is one major reason why marine fish and freshwater fish will not generally survive in each other's environment. The process by which the salts are absorbed and excreted from the fish's body and the way in which they control their salt levels is known as osmoregulation.

How osmoregulation works

In all fish there is a natural difference between the level of salts found in the fish's body fluids and the level of salts in the surrounding environment, whether it is freshwater or saltwater. Only very thin membranes, such as the gills, separate the differing levels, so there is a tendency for water and salts to flow constantly into and out of the fish. This two-way movement is caused by diffusion and osmosis, natural processes that occur wherever two solutions of different concentrations are separated by a partially permeable membrane. The salt ions move from the more concentrated solution through the membrane and into the weaker solution; this is diffusion. The water molecules will move in the opposite

Below: Scats (Scatophagus argus) *are one of the few species that can live in a range of salinities, from near freshwater to marine conditions. They can rapidly adjust their osmoregulation to cope.*

Freshwater osmoregulation

Water passes by osmosis from the relatively dilute freshwater into the fish's body.

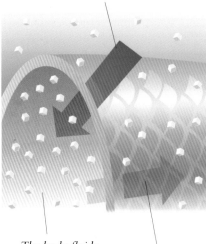

The body fluids have a higher salt concentration than the surrounding water.

Salts pass out by diffusion.

Kidneys excrete water and retain salts.

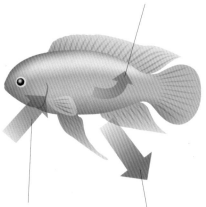

Chloride cells in the gills retain salts from water flowing over them.

Large amounts of very dilute urine are produced.

Saltwater osmoregulation

Water passes by osmosis from the relatively dilute fish's body out into the sea.

The body fluids have a lower salt concentration than the surrounding water.

Salts pass in by diffusion.

Water, but not salts, absorbed in gut.

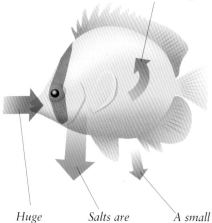

Huge quantities of water are swallowed.

Salts are actively eliminated by the gills.

A small amount of urine is produced.

direction and dilute the stronger solution; this is osmosis.

Marine fish differ from their freshwater relatives in the way they balance the levels of salts and fluids in their bodies. The bodies of freshwater fish contain a higher level of salts than the surrounding water. There is a tendency for salts to be lost through the tissues as water flows in. To combat this, freshwater fish have extremely efficient kidneys that are able to excrete water very quickly, while retaining the salts in

Below: Seawater contains a high level of dissolved salts and marine life is adapted to thrive in this salty environment.
Keeping marine creatures successfully in a tank is made easier today by using synthetic mixes that reflect the natural salt balance of the sea.

the water by reabsorbing them from the urine. Additionally, freshwater fish have specially structured gills that allow them to retain salts circulating in the blood that have been ingested with food.

In marine fish the situation is reversed. Their environment has a higher salt level than is found in their body fluids. As a result, they face a constant battle against dehydration, as water is lost to the surrounding seawater and salts are retained in the body. Marine fish deal with this situation by consuming large amounts of water and excreting very little urine. Only a few salts are absorbed from the seawater they drink and special chloride cells in the gills actively excrete salt.

Types of marine fish

There are two types of marine fish: those with cartilaginous skeletons, such as sharks and rays, and those with a bony skeleton. There are several key differences in the body shape and fins that indicate whether a species is cartilaginous or bony, and it is mainly the latter type of fish that we are concerned with as hobbyists.

Body shape

Marine fishes of all types have adapted to live in their surroundings. Just looking at the exterior shape and features of a fish will provide many clues to where it lives, how it feeds and what it feeds on. Body shape is thus a good indication of the 'lifestyle' of a fish. This variation is part of the attraction of keeping a range of species in an aquarium.

Laterally compressed fish are found in two forms. Flatfish, such as plaice and flounders, look flat – as though they have been squashed from above. They live on the seabed, lying on their sides. Both the eyes are on the 'top surface' (one migrates around the head) so that the fishes have good vision in their resting position.

Fish such as angelfish and surgeonfish are compressed from side to side and swim in the normal orientation. Although they do not swim as rapidly as more streamlined fish, their shape allows them to manoeuvre deftly between the corals and reef faces that they inhabit.

Most fish are laterally compressed to some degree. Those with a more streamlined shape – correctly known as fusiforms – are extremely fast swimmers that usually live in open waters. Typified by species such as tuna and barracuda, these fish are often seen shoaling, and many are

Above: The flattened shape and enlarged pectoral fins of this stingray are ideal for its bottom-dwelling way of life. Like their relatives, the sharks, rays have a skeleton made of cartilage rather than bone.

predatory, relying on speed through the water to catch their quarry.

Vertically compressed fish may appear to be the same as some laterally compressed fish, but differ in that they are truly flattened and do not lie on their sides. Stingrays are typical examples of vertically compressed fish. These bottom-dwellers blend in with their sandy surroundings and capture prey by relying on camouflage and a quick burst of speed rather than by pursuit.

Snakelike fish, such as the wide variety of eels found in the oceans, are perfectly shaped to suit their environment. Eels are able to move rapidly within the tight nooks and crannies found on the reefs, and they can anchor their muscular bodies to rocks, pouncing on their unsuspecting prey. Their flexibility is partly due to the way in which their skeletons, in particular the vertebrae making up the backbone, have developed over time.

Many fish do not fall into any particular shape category. Their distinctive appearances are often due to natural defence mechanisms, as with the spiny puffer, or with the need for efficient camouflage in order to catch their prey, perfectly demonstrated by the anglerfish.

How fish move through the water

Water is almost 800 times denser than air and this presents problems for any moving object. To move forwards, a fish has to propel water backwards along its body, but does not have two or four legs with which to 'push off'. Fish body shapes and muscle groups have evolved to cope with their dense environment. They

Below: Many of the fish that live around the coral outcrops of a tropical reef have laterally compressed body shapes. This enables them to swim into confined spaces to reach small food items or to scrape algae from the rock surfaces.

swim by passing a series of waves down the flanks of the body. These waves increase in size at the same time as the head moves from side to side. The combined actions cause the fish to 'snake' through the water. Of course, there are exceptions to this rule and some fish, such as the boxfish, rely only on small movements at the base of the tail to move them along.

The undulating action of most fish is only possible because of the flexibility of their spines. The number and size of vertebrae in the spine affect the flexibility of a fish. For example, a boxfish may have 14 vertebrae, while snakelike eels may have up to 100, giving them far greater flexibility.

The functions of the fins

The fins perform the same function as the limbs of land animals. They are connected to powerful sets of

Above: The fusiform body shape and forked tail of these barracudas are typical of streamlined fish 'designed' for fast swimming in open water. Juveniles stay together in shoals, whereas lone adults of larger species are solitary hunters.

muscles and used for propulsion, manoeuvring and sometimes even for protection. They consist mainly of a thin patch of skin, supported by a framework of very fine bony rays. If damaged, fins generally regenerate quickly, as long as infection has not set in. The fin rays can also regrow, although they may be distorted if they have been partially broken.

Different species have evolved fins to suit their own environment, and the shape and number of fins varies between species. However, they usually include some paired fins, such as the pectoral and pelvic fins, and some unpaired fins such as the anal, caudal and dorsal fins.

Paired fins are used for manoeuvring, both laterally or vertically. Many species also use them during breeding, both in display and, later, to fan water over eggs and fry, thus ensuring a regular flow of oxygenated water past the brood.

Some fish use their pectoral fins to dig in the sandy sea bottom, while others appear to sit up on their fins, looking for food and predators.

Pectoral fins can rotate and are extended out from the body for use as brakes, when quick deceleration is required. With the pectoral fins extended, there would be a tendency

for the fish to pitch upwards or downwards, were it not for the pelvic fins, which act as stabilizers to keep the fish level. As well as being used for propulsion and braking, the pectorals can also be used to maintain a fish's position in a current of water, enabling the fish to 'hover' over a potential food source or point of refuge.

Unpaired fins – or median fins as they are more correctly known – are found in the centre of a fish's vertical axis. The dorsal fin, located along the top of the fish, is in line with the

The fins and what they do

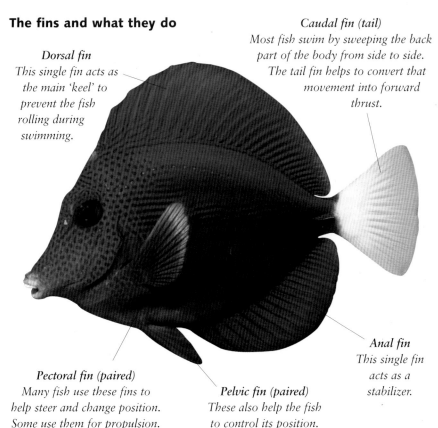

Dorsal fin
This single fin acts as the main 'keel' to prevent the fish rolling during swimming.

Caudal fin (tail)
Most fish swim by sweeping the back part of the body from side to side. The tail fin helps to convert that movement into forward thrust.

Pectoral fin (paired)
Many fish use these fins to help steer and change position. Some use them for propulsion.

Pelvic fin (paired)
These also help the fish to control its position.

Anal fin
This single fin acts as a stabilizer.

Above: Blennies appear to perch on their pelvic fins, often on corals and rocks, on the lookout for food. This is a redlipped blenny (Ophioblennius atlanticus).

forward movement of the fish, acting like a keel on a boat. It is balanced by the anal fin, which, as its name suggests, is found just behind a fish's vent. Together they prevent the fish from rolling laterally.

Some species, such as the lionfish, have poisonous spines in their fins and will adopt a 'head-down' stance, with the spines pointing outwards, if they feel threatened.

The caudal fin, or tail, varies greatly in marine fish species, and its shape can be a clue to the type of environment inhabited by the fish.

Tail shapes

There are three basic tail shapes that can be a useful guide to a fish's speed. This in turn may be an indication of its natural habitat and can lead to a greater understanding of how to maintain the fish in the aquarium. There are many fish, such as the ribbon eel, that have no visible caudal fin; they propel themselves by scything their bodies through the water, with similar movements to those used by snakes.

Forked tail A forked tail can help to create a high level of manoeuvrability and is often seen in predatory open-water fish. The streamlined form of the tail helps the fish move through the water at high speeds.

Crescent tail Many aquarium fish
have crescent tails, their tail shape
helping them to manoeuvre easily
among coral reefs. The muscles in
the tail region help these fish to
control direction, even in the surging
water flow around an inshore reef.

Rounded tail Fish with rounded tails
are usually poor swimmers. They are
likely to be slow-moving fish that
rarely stray far from the reef, where
they can seek refuge in crevices or, in
the case of clownfishes, in the
embrace of a suitable anemone. They
are unlikely to chase their prey, but
many ambush passing 'food'.

The mouth

The shape and size of a marine fish's
mouth may give an indication of its
diet, thus helping you to avoid
making expensive mistakes when
choosing species for the aquarium.

One look at the extended jaw of a
lionfish should be enough to tell you
that anything that will fit inside it is
likely to be devoured. Triggerfish, on
the other hand, have fairly small,
slightly pointed mouths with visible,
tiny, sharp teeth. These hard-nosed
fish devour shelled crustaceans, and
have even adapted to eating prickly
starfish, by first blowing them onto
their backs and then devouring the
soft underside. Needless to say,
triggerfish are not ideal subjects for
an aquarium containing corals,
starfishes and other invertebrates.

Fish such as the longnose
butterflyfish *(Forcipiger longirostris)*
have specialized feeding habits, and
their long snouts enable them to pick

Tail fin shapes

*Forked tails are typical
of fast predatory fish such as
barracudas and trevallies. The deeper
the fork, the more likely the fish is to
be a fast swimmer.*

*Crescent, or lyre-shaped, tails are
common in reef fish. A classic example
is the wreckfish* (Pseudanthias
squamipinnis), *also known as
the lyretail anthias.*

*Round tails, here on a
clownfish, are typical of fish
that live close to the reef.*

algae and food morsels from deep within the heads of corals. The small, delicate nature of this type of mouth indicates that the fish is almost certainly not a threat to other species.

Bone structure

With the exception of the cartilaginous species, such as sharks and rays, all fish have a bony skeleton. This provides a strong base around which muscle and other body tissues can form. The skeleton is basically in three sections: the skull, the spine (backbone), and the skeletal supports for the delicate fin rays.

Below: Using its small mouth armed with teeth, this moon wrasse (Thalassoma lunare) *greedily consumes invertebrates, including crabs and molluscs. Wrasses will move rocks aside to reach food.*

The skull provides protection for the brain, as well as housing the eyes and other sense organs. Muscles and tissue around the gills and jaws are also fixed to the small bones that make up the structure of the skull.

The spine is a column of bones connected by ligaments that allow it to flex. Without this ability, a fish would not be able to swim. Fish have a series of ribs that provide some protection to the vital internal organs. The spine also contains the spinal cord, which passes through a canal formed by the bony arches of

Right: This head-on view of a lionfish (Pterois volitans) *clearly shows the wide mouth that will rapidly engulf any smaller fish that it has ambushed. The fin spines are poisonous for defence.*

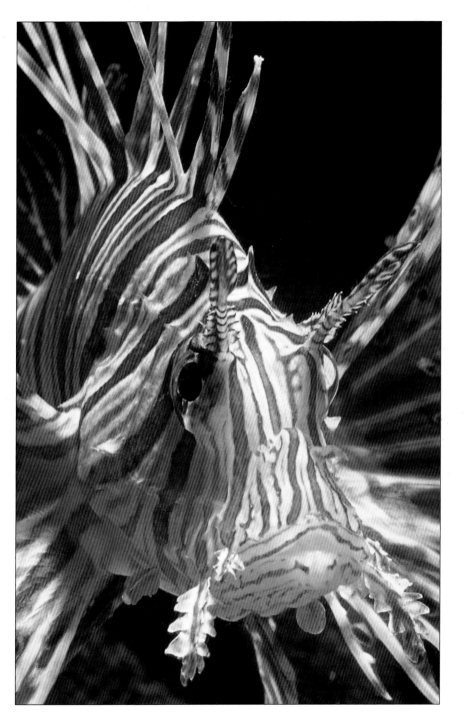

the vertebrae and into the skull. The spinal cord is made up of nerve fibres that connect the brain to the sense organs and all parts of the body.

The scales

As well as a layer of skin, most marine fish have a covering of scales, which not only help protect the fish against damage, but also make the fish streamlined, so that it can move through water more easily. In most fish, the scales overlap in a similar way to roof tiles, reducing drag through the water. The overlapping scales give the muscles room to move in a way that provides propulsion, as we have discussed on page 28.

Scales grow with a fish, but are quite delicate. While they can regenerate if damaged, they are not always sufficient to protect the fish against abrasions caused by sharp rocks around the reef, where the water flow can be surging and hostile. Fish inhabiting the surge areas of a reef often have a thicker skin to provide protection.

Some fish have tough, spiny scales to deter predators. Fish such as the spiny boxfish are covered in scales with spines that can be raised as the fish inflates. The drawback is the additional weight and the reduced flexibility, which combine to make such fish slow and clumsy swimmers.

The internal anatomy

Although the shapes, sizes and colours of marine fish vary enormously, their internal anatomy is based on a common template. Here, we look inside them in more detail.

The gills

Fish require oxygen, but do not come to the surface of the ocean to inhale. Instead, they 'breathe' underwater, using a finely adapted method of removing essential oxygen from the water. This invaluable gas is used to convert nutrients into energy and growth potential, but is far harder to extract from water than from air, which contains about 40 times more oxygen per cubic metre. To extract oxygen effectively, water is forced over extremely fine blood capillaries, where oxygen can quickly be absorbed by the haemoglobin in the blood. This action takes place in the gills, which also help in the release of toxic carbon dioxide into the water.

In most marine fish, water enters the mouth and passes through the gills, where oxygen is extracted by the delicate filaments. To aid absorption, these gill filaments are made up of huge numbers of tiny leaflike fronds, known as lamellae.

To prevent oxygen diffusing out of the blood capillaries, water flows across the gills in the opposite direction to the flow of blood in the lamellae. This process, known as the counter-current principle, ensures that at whatever point blood and water come into contact with each other, the water has a higher oxygen content than the blood. Oxygen-depleted blood entering the lamellae will initially meet water from which some oxygen has already been extracted, while blood high in oxygen, and exiting the lamellae, will meet with water entering the lamellae, and thus high in oxygen.

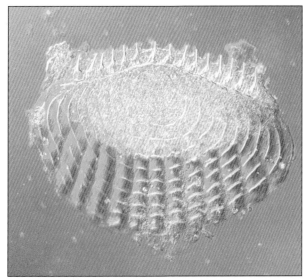

Left: Scales are easily damaged by incorrect handling. They are the protective outer skin, and are intricately formed to help the fish move effortlessly through water.

Below: Pufferfish exploit the nature of their scalation and inflate themselves with water to deter the attentions of any would-be predators.

Basic internal anatomy

Marine fish are delicate creatures and it is vital to learn what makes them tick, and why and how they live where they do. Greater understanding increases the chance of setting up a successful aquarium.

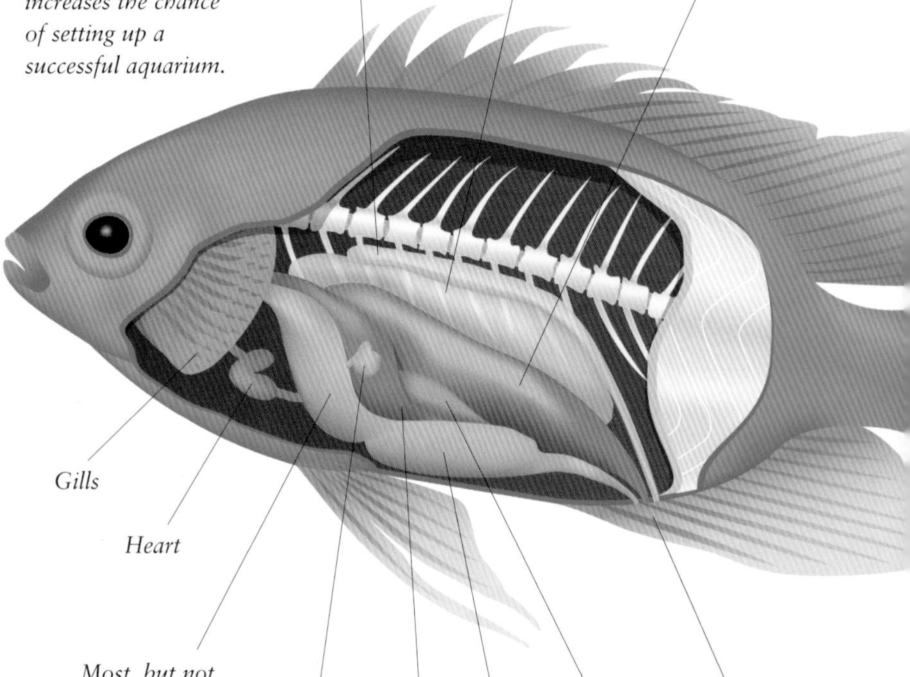

The kidneys help to control the amount of water retained in the body and play a role in immune function.

The swimbladder provides buoyancy. In most fishes, the gas inside is mainly oxygen.

This is the position of the reproductive organs. The ovary and testes produce eggs and sperm (milt) respectively and these pass to the vent.

Gills

Heart

Most, but not all, fish have a stomach, where food is stored and digestion begins.

Gall bladder

Liver

Partially digested food is passed from the stomach into the intestines, where it is broken down and the nutritious content absorbed.

Spleen

Waste is expelled through separate openings from the gut and kidneys. Eggs and sperm (milt) also arrive at this area, called the vent.

The counter-current principle greatly increases the efficiency of the gills in their role as oxygen gatherers.

Water does not simply flow into the mouth and over the gills. With the gill covers closed, the fish sucks in water through the mouth, closes it and then forces the water, under pressure, over the gills and out of the now open gill covers.

The swimbladder

The weight of a fish's skeleton creates negative buoyancy, so that there is a natural tendency for it to sink. This is countered by the swimbladder, control of which dictates the level in the water at which the fish swims.

The pressure of water increases by one atmosphere (literally the normal air pressure in the atmosphere) for every 10 metres descended. This in turn has an effect on fish with gaseous swimbladders, as gases become compressed as pressure increases. Due to the difference in densities between air, water and the fish's tissue, between 5 and 7 percent of the fish's volume must be filled with either air or gas for the fish to

How the swimbladder works

Above: As a fish rises, outside pressure decreases and the natural tendency is for the swimbladder to inflate as the gas inside expands. To maintain neutral buoyancy, some gas is absorbed back into the bloodstream, thus deflating the swimbladder so that the volume of gas remains constant.

Above: As a fish descends, outside pressure increases and the natural tendency is for the swimbladder to deflate as the gas inside is compressed. To maintain neutral buoyancy, gas passes from the bloodstream into the swimbladder, thus inflating it so that the volume of gas remains constant.

reach equilibrium. While this works in shallow water, the gas becomes compressed at depth, causing the fish to sink. To remedy this, the swimbladder is inflated during descent and deflated when the fish rises. In this way, the volume of gas will be kept at the same level despite compression, as the pressure inside the swimbladder is the same as that of the surrounding water.

The swimbladder is an essential part of the fish's anatomy, as it allows the fish to remain stable in the water column. Situated below the backbone and the kidneys (see page 36), the swimbladder extends from the gut and in development is connected to it via a small duct. Marine fishes tend to have a swimbladder with a closed duct.

Below: Sharks, such as these blacktip reef sharks (Carcharhinus melanopterus) *use their senses of smell, vibration-detection, and sensitivity to weak electric fields.*

The muscles

Muscles enable the fins and mouth to operate, and they control all the major body movements. Fish have two types of muscle: oxygen-rich red muscle and oxygen-poor muscle, known as white muscle.

Red muscle gets its coloration from myoglobin – a form of haemoglobin. The high oxygen content in red muscle enables it to be used for continual swimming and manoeuvring, and is prominent in open-water feeding fish that constantly cruise around, often over large areas. White muscle, which functions anaerobically (without oxygen), can only be used for very short periods, and is usually employed when a fish requires an extra burst of speed.

The senses

Like any other animal, fish need to assess their environment constantly for sources of food, danger and

How a fish's eye works

Unlike land animals, fish focus by moving the lens rather than squeezing it to change its shape. Forward vision is sharper than to the sides.

The cornea – a thin sandwich of transparent layers.

The retina converts images into nerve impulses.

The lens remains roughly spherical at all focus ranges.

The optic nerve carries these 'images' to the brain.

Blood supply to the retina.

This muscle moves the lens to and fro in the direction of the head and tail to focus images on the retina.

The falciform process distributes blood around the retina.

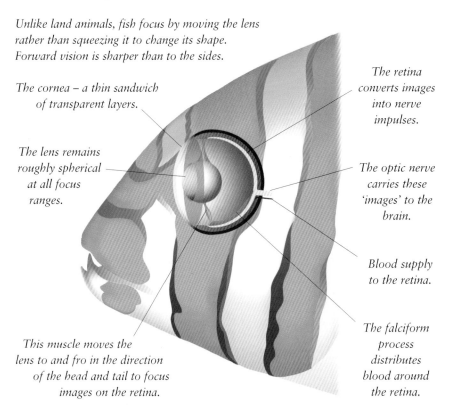

breeding potential. If conditions are not adequate, the fish must be prepared to move on to a different area. Factors contributing to the assessment of a particular area include temperature, pressure, water quality, water current, sound, vibrations and odour. The need for senses to detect all these parameters varies between species, depending on their requirements. Sharks, for example, have an extremely heightened sense of smell that enables them to smell blood from huge distances, although their eyesight is not particularly strong.

Sight

Eyesight is probably perceived as the most important sense for humans, and we are certainly the poorer if we lose it. Our eyes are prominent, large, and well protected in bony sockets. They are positioned to give maximum binocular sight. Eyesight in fishes is also important, but the levels of turbidity around a reef or the lack of light in deep water regions means that eyesight tends to be supplemented by other senses more suited to the environment. Patterns and colour play an important part in a fish's life, whether for courtship or concealment, which indicates that fish have reasonable vision.

Experiments have been done to prove that fish can see colour. They have been trained to respond to certain colour disks that indicate that they are to be fed. Studies of a fish's eye show that in the retina there are two types of cell: rods and cones.

Both contain pigments that react to light in different ways. The rod cells give fish the ability to see fine detail, and, as might be expected, are heightened in fish living in dimly lit waters. The cone cells are responsible for colour perception and only function in bright light.

In fish living on the reef, there is a balance of rods and cones that allows

A predatory fish's visual field

The eyes are positioned high on the head, relatively close together.

The peripheral vision is limited, due to the position of the eyes on the head.

Forward vision is excellent and allows the fish to seek its prey and hunt it, even in murky water.

A non-predatory fish's visual field

The eyes are positioned on the side of the head.

Peripheral vision is excellent and the fish can feed while remaining vigilant for predators.

Forward field of view is not as wide and sharp, but this is not critical because their food is usually non-moving.

them to recognize mates, rivals, prey and predators. However, species living in deeper waters have a lower ratio of cones to rods; indeed, in many deepwater fish, the cones are completely absent.

Fish can focus on close and distant objects, and can also see above the water surface. Any fisherman who has stalked a trout will know that keeping out of sight is essential, and fish such as the brackish water archerfish feed from insects far above in branches, shooting them down with jets of water.

Eye placement, and the consequent field of vision, depends largely on the requirements of a particular species. For example, non-predatory fish, such as tangs and butterflyfishes, have eyes in the side of the head. This gives them a wide field of vision, albeit perhaps with a slightly less sharp rendition. This wide field of vision alerts the fish to danger, as it can see a predator approaching from almost any angle. However, fish such as groupers have forward-facing eyes placed high on the head. Their field of vision is reduced but better defined, and they are able to see prey at greater distances in the forward view.

Hearing

Because of the greater density of water, sound travels through it much further and up to five times faster than it does through air.

Fish sense sound as pressure waves and have evolved to make the most of their heightened hearing methods. Sounds resulting from high-frequency vibrations can indicate the presence of prey or predators, and enable a fish to gauge the geography and layout of an area of reef or ocean. All these factors are of vital importance to fish, which have two systems to detect these sounds.

The ears lie in paired cavities towards the back of the skull. Importantly, this is near the fulcrum, or most stable point, of a fish's body when it moves. The ease with which sound and vibrations penetrate water has negated the requirement for fish to have middle and external ears, and only the inner ear is developed.

The ear cavity is divided into two parts: the upper utriculus and the lower sacculus. Only the lower part is used for hearing, and fish can detect sound waves of up to 8,000 Herz (cycles per second). Humans can detect 10,000 Herz, and bats 100,000 Herz. The ability of sharks to detect sound vibrations is well documented; they can 'hear' a struggling fish from several hundred metres. If removed from the water, several species of fish emit a startling array of sounds, from clicks to whistles. These sounds may be distress calls or an indication of threatening behaviour, but they all indicate the importance of sound and hearing on the reef.

The lateral line is the fish's other means of detecting sounds. It is clearly visible as a row of small 'dots' along the flanks of most species. These dots are pores leading to a canal dotted with sensory hair cells.

Above: With prominent tubular nostrils, moray eels have
a superb sense of smell and use it to good effect when
detecting prey. They remain partly hidden in a crevice
until suitable prey passes within grabbing distance.

Differences in water pressure caused by vibrations affect the hair cells, which send signals to the brain. The lateral line can sense low-frequency vibrations – about 200 Herz – which suggests that it is mainly used for echo-sounding (as used by bats), enabling the fish to 'see' in the dark.

Smell and taste

Fish differ from land animals in the way they detect smell and taste. On land, smell and taste are distinguished by the way in which the sense organs are stimulated. However, in oceans and rivers, both smell and taste can only be detected as a result of substances being dissolved in the water. Fish have paired nostrils in front of the eyes, as well as sensory cells in the mouth and gills, and these provide them with a sense of smell that is one million times more sensitive than that of humans.

Often, it is species with poor eyesight that have the best sense of smell, since they must find their food without visual help. As well as using smell to locate food, fish also excrete 'odour messages' called pheromones to communicate with other fish.

Colour, pattern and camouflage

Colour is possibly the main reason for the popularity of marine fishkeeping. Although there are some vibrant, colourful examples of freshwater fish, there is no doubt that the sheer diversity of startling colours and patterns seen in marine fishes across the world is unmatched by their freshwater relatives.

Colour in marine fish is mainly produced by pigment cells in the body. These cells exist in a mixture of black, yellow and red forms, and together make up the wide varieties of colours witnessed on the reef. Some fish have direct control over their pigmentation and can change their colour at will.

It may seem strange to us that a large proportion of marine fishes are bright red and orange. Surely these stunning blocks of colour are not suited to small fish that must avoid detection by predatory species? In fact, in the underwater world, red is an ideal colour for camouflage. Most red-coloured fish either inhabit fairly deep waters, where light levels are low, or are nocturnal. In deep water, red is quickly filtered out, rendering the fish grey in appearance. Anyone who has dived on a coral reef will have noticed that the colours are far more subdued in reality than they seem under the artificial lighting necessary for video or film images.

Many marine fish are bicoloured, often light on the underside and dark on the upper body. As with red coloration, this actually helps the fish to remain inconspicuous. When viewed from the side in an aquarium, these fish appear to stand out and are often popular aquarium inhabitants for this very reason. However, in their natural environment, these fish appear dark when viewed from above, blending in with the darker water below them. When viewed from below, their light shading helps them to blend into the lighter water above them. In fact, some seabirds have a similar coloration to help camouflage them as they dive below the waves in pursuit of fish.

Warning colours are used by many species of fish to deter predators. Surgeonfish and tangs often have bright spots near the tail in order to highlight the sharp spines. Other fish use bright splashes of colour to highlight the presence of poisonous spines, and squid are famous for their ability to change colour, chameleon-like, to display aggression and other emotions.

With many predators prowling on the reef, shoaling together as blocks of colour can help smaller fishes to confuse an attacker. The solid coloration of a shoal makes it more difficult for a larger fish to pick out one single fish as prey. And as the shoal swirls, sudden changes in shape can be dazzling, as light catches the

Right: Many fish seek protection in numbers. Being part of a large shoal, such as these Moorish idols (Zanclus canescens), reduces the chances of individuals being caught as prey.

different angles of the fishes' bodies, distracting the predator and allowing the fish to escape.

The amazing patterns of marine fish are also not immediately obvious sources of disguise and camouflage. Often, these fish are seen in bare aquariums, with only rock and other fish for company. However, in their natural environment, with a backdrop of vividly coloured corals, even fish as striking as the Moorish idol *(Zanclus canescens)* blend into their surroundings. This disruptive patterning is similar to that seen in zebras, giraffes and many big cat species on the African plains.

Left: The bizarre-looking frogfish (Antennarius sp.) relies on camouflage to remain undetected as it waits for passing prey. These and the related anglerfishes attract their prey by dangling a lure formed from the first few rays of the dorsal fin over their capacious, 'hair-trigger' mouths.

HOW MARINE FISH BREED

The demand for supplies of fish other than from the wild has led to far more research into the reproductive behaviour of marine fishes and will, in time, result in many more species being successfully spawned and raised in captivity.

In the past, marine fish were readily available to the hobbyist straight from their wild habitat, but today the situation is changing. There is far more emphasis on sustainable exporting of species and several countries have instigated a breeding and reintroduction programme to bolster natural stocks, depleted not by hobbyists, but by commercial overfishing and pollution.

Unlike freshwater fishes, many of which are easy to breed in a home aquarium, very few species of marine fish have been successfully spawned.

Eggs on board

The male red-banded pipefish *(Doryhamphus dactyliophorus)* carries eggs in a line slung beneath its elongated body.

Nor has it been possible to raise the subsequent fry. This lack of success in domestic breeding can be partly attributed to the fact that in an average-sized aquarium, many marine fish cannot be housed together with another of their species without fighting. For example, angelfish and surgeons will fight with any fish that even resembles their own species, so selecting a breeding pair and giving them space in which to perform courtship rituals is almost impossible.

Types of spawning

The breeding habits of marine fish are, perhaps, surprisingly similar. This is explained by the lack of differing habitats available to them. For example, some freshwater fish occupy quiet, undisturbed waters where they can build delicate bubblenests, while others can bury their eggs and leave them to incubate for several months. However, the breeding habits of the majority of marine fish do not lend themselves well to the confines of an aquarium.

Columnar and group spawnings

Many species, including the large butterflyfish and angelfish families, reportedly perform a rapid, spiral ascent towards the water surface, releasing eggs and sperm into the water column. As most aquariums are relatively shallow, this behaviour is not possible in captivity. Another aspect of spawning behaviour that is impossible to replicate in an aquarium is that of seasonal group spawnings. Some species, especially of open water fish, gather annually for mass group spawnings. These fish do not mate for life, but are opportunistic breeders, picking a mate at random, for a one-off encounter.

Egg depositors

Species that deposit their eggs, rather than scatter them, are generally easier to breed in an aquarium. These include damselfish, hawkfish and gobies, as well as the best-known of all marine fish, the clown, or

Below: An adult French angelfish (Pomacanthus paru) *near a wreck. This and other large angelfish and butterflyfish scatter their fertilized eggs near the surface after an ascending spawning display.*

anemonefish. These species have been bred successfully for many years and are commercially bred in many countries. Egg depositors lay many sticky eggs on a flat surface, such as a piece of rock or coral skeleton. For example, damselfish often spawn in small caves, laying their eggs on the underside of the cave roof. In the wild, clownfish spawn around the security of their host anemone. Although they may be bred without an anemone, the chances of success are greatly increased by understanding their natural behaviour and trying to replicate it as closely as possible in an aquarium.

Mouthbrooders
Mouthbrooders, such as the yellow-headed jawfish *(Opistognathus aurifrons)*, incubate their eggs in the adult male's mouth. When they are capable of swimming, the fry are ejected, but the adult's mouth remains a refuge in times of danger, and the fry are seldom allowed to stray far from their parents in their formative weeks.

Pouch brooders
Along with the clownfish, the most often spawned species of fish is the seahorse, whose young are incubated in a pouch on the male's abdomen. (This pouch is external to the body

Left: The yellow-headed jawfish (Opistognathus aurifrons) *briefly away from its burrow, reveals its delicately coloured body. In this species, the male incubates the fertilized eggs in its mouth. Aquarium breeding has been successful.*

and therefore seahorses are not considered to be 'livebearers'.) Using a small tube called an ovipositor, the female, places the eggs in the pouch, where the male incubates them for up to two months. The young seahorses are then born as perfectly formed miniatures of their parents.

This unique method of incubation provides fascinating viewing for hobbyists who decide to keep this delicate species.

Species for aquarium breeding
When presented with the evidence, you might think that achieving breeding success with marine fish is a lost cause. However, the news is not all bad and there are some species of fish that can be successfully spawned and raised in captivity with a little effort. Here we look at two marine fish species that can be successfully bred and offer some general guidance on raising the resulting fry. The methods described here are by no means the only way to breed these species, but they are known to yield reasonably successful results.

Preparation is vital
Before undertaking to breed any fish or invertebrates, give some thought to where and how you will accommodate the young. Once you have mastered the basics of spawning various species, you will be faced with the challenge of what to do with 30-40, or even 100 growing fish. If adult fish spawn naturally in your home aquarium, it is unlikely that many, if any, of the resulting fry will survive. However, if the objective

is to raise the fry through to adulthood, you may well need to negotiate with your local aquatic shop before you run out of room in your house!

Breeding clownfishes
Clownfishes are probably the most frequently captive-bred marine fish, and one of the few that can be viably bred commercially.

The life of a clownfish revolves around a small area surrounding the host anemone. Living in an aquarium does not greatly inhibit its territorial requirements, unlike other species that need hundreds of metres of open sea in which to roam. As commercially bred fish do not usually have even a host anemone, it is not surprising that a pair of clownfish in a natural-looking aquarium should regularly spawn.

Selecting a pair
There are two simple ways of selecting a suitable pair. Either buy a guaranteed pair from your aquatic supplier or buy a group of juvenile clownfish (five or six should suffice) and watch their behaviour as they grow. This method requires more patience but can be extremely rewarding. Look for a pair that show interest in each other and are of different sizes. The female clownfish is always larger than the male and

Right: A pair of common clownfish (Amphiprion ocellaris) guard the eggs they have laid on a tile in their otherwise bare tank. In the wild, they clean a flat rock surface on which to lay their eggs.

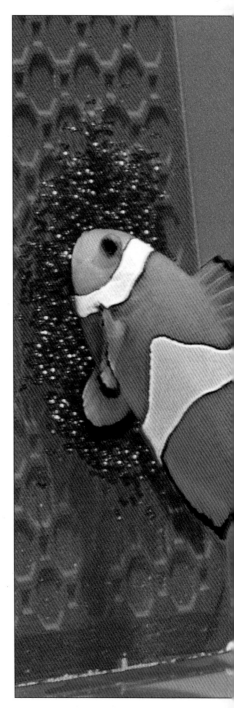

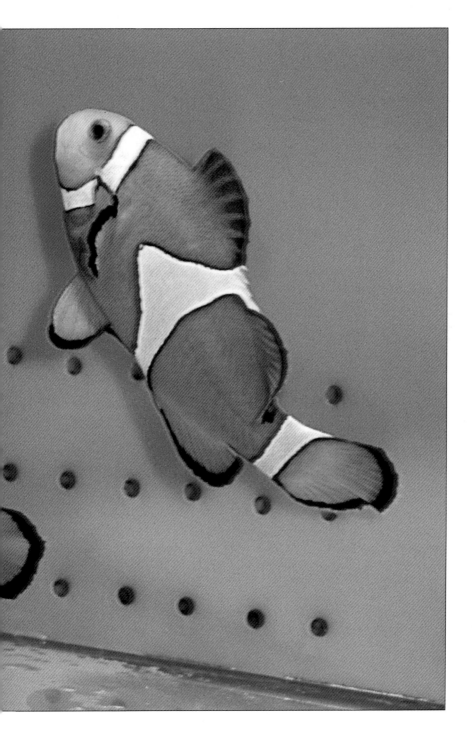

A clownfish breeding tank

Ideally, the breeding tank should be as natural as possible to allow the parent fish to settle in. However, you can succeed with a sparsely furnished aquarium as shown here.

Remove the adults and slate once the fry are free swimming.

Install a simple bubble-up sponge filter.

Provide a flat surface such as a piece of slate for the eggs to be laid on.

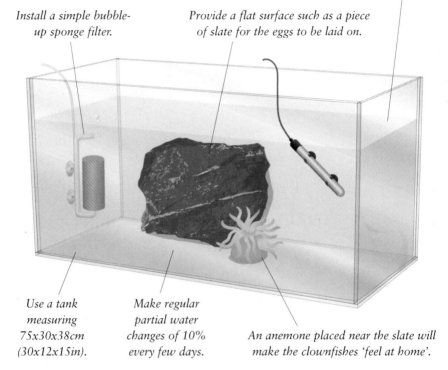

Use a tank measuring 75x30x38cm (30x12x15in).

Make regular partial water changes of 10% every few days.

An anemone placed near the slate will make the clownfishes 'feel at home'.

he, as the dominant male, will in turn be larger than the other clownfish in the group.

All clownfish start life as males. This strategy may have developed from their challenging start to life in the wild, where newly hatched clownfish drift with the plankton until they find a host anemone with clownfish of the same species already 'in residence'. The successful fry will be 'adopted' by the resident adults and will spend their juvenile life around the extended family. When the resident adult female clownfish dies – clownfish can live for up to 12-15 years – the breeding male develops into a female and one of the adopted juvenile fish takes on the role of the active male. This chain of events ensures that the anemone has a constant resident population of breeding fish, as well as ensuring that fresh genes are introduced into the clownfish community with every generation change.

Clownfish often spawn on a rocky surface within the protective reach of the host anemone's tentacles. First, the site is thoroughly cleaned, a sure sign of impending egglaying. After a spawning has taken place, it is usually five to seven days before the large yellow eggs hatch into larval fry. When the eggs have hatched, the tiny fry will head for the surface of the aquarium, where they will continue to live off their yolk sacs.

Feeding clownfish fry

Once a successful spawning has been achieved, the hard work is only just beginning, as the fry require regular feeding and maintenance.

Freshwater fish are relatively easy to feed from an early age and a number of proprietary foods are available. Marine fish, on the other hand, require special foods, many of which, such as rotifers, require some time, effort and planning to produce. The 7-14 days that clownfish spend in their larval stage are absolutely crucial. Once the fry have used up the proteins in their yolk sac, they require a regular supply of cultured rotifers. These tiny invertebrates feed from algae and can be grown from cultures available from aquatic shops. A constant supply of rotifers is required until the fry are large enough to accept newly hatched brineshrimp. At this stage, most of the difficulties are over, and it should be possible to raise the remaining fry successfully. As they grow, they will require exceptional water quality and a regular supply of frozen and live foods in order to progress.

Breeding seahorses

Seahorses are a fascinating family of fish. However, before undertaking to keep them, you should do some careful research to make sure that you will be able to maintain these delicate creatures. Contrary to popular belief, seahorses are not easy to keep and many die of starvation, despite eating all the food they are offered. It is not enough simply to feed them frozen brineshrimp; you must be prepared to offer them a variety of suitable foods, including mysis shrimps, live gammarus shrimps and river shrimp. The advent of cryogenic freezing and Omega-3 enhancement of frozen brineshrimp has greatly added to its suitability as a food source for seahorses.

An alternative strategy is to keep tropical freshwater fish, such as mollies and guppies, in a separate tank and use their young as a diet for seahorses, but this depends upon your view of feeding live foods.

A seahorse aquarium

Seahorses need a quiet aquarium, away from fast-swimming or boisterous fish. It need not be large, but must have an abundance of hiding places and anchor points. Artificial gorgonians are ideal for the adult seahorses to wrap their tails around while they pick at passing food. Ensure that any air bubbles, such as those from a protein skimmer or diffuser, are kept out of reach of seahorses, as they often mistake small bubbles for food. Swallowing air bubbles can cause serious health problems and must be avoided.

Given the correct food and a suitable aquarium, seahorses are relatively easy to breed and their young are somewhat less demanding to raise than those of other marine fishes. Seahorses have a unique and well-documented method of reproduction.

After a courtship often lasting for two to three days, during which the colour is intensified in both sexes, the female uses her ovipositor tube to deposit the eggs into a pouch at the front of the male's abdomen. They are then fertilised by the male, who incubates them for up to two months. Once the young have hatched (as perfectly formed miniatures of their parents), they are independent and the parents take no further role in raising their offspring. The young seahorses usually head straight for the top of the tank, where they fill their airbladders. Under no circumstances should they ever be removed from the water. If you transfer them to a growing-on tank, do this extremely carefully, ensuring that you keep the seahorses submerged at all times to prevent them gulping air in the process.

Below: A male seahorse with its abdominal pouch swollen with fertilized eggs. They will stay there for two months before breaking out as free-swimming fry.

Feeding seahorse fry

Ideally, establish an algae and plankton culture on which to feed the young in the initial few days. This can be a somewhat lengthy procedure, but it does yield more successful results than relying on newly hatched brineshrimp. If you are thinking of breeding seahorses, it is a good idea to seek the advice of your marine aquarium retailer on how and where to buy plankton kits.

Alternatively, feed the young seahorses on freshly hatched brineshrimp or even frozen baby brineshrimp. Seahorses need constant supplies of food, another reason why algae and plankton are a better food than brineshrimp, which can be quickly filtered out of the aquarium.

Once the young are large enough, offer them them the same mixture of foods as their parents in order to provide a nutritionally balanced diet.

A seahorse breeding tank

A fairly sparse tank setup is fine for breeding seahorses. It is vital to maintain good water quality.

Use an external canister filter containing mature biological filter media.

Make regular partial water changes of 10% every few days.

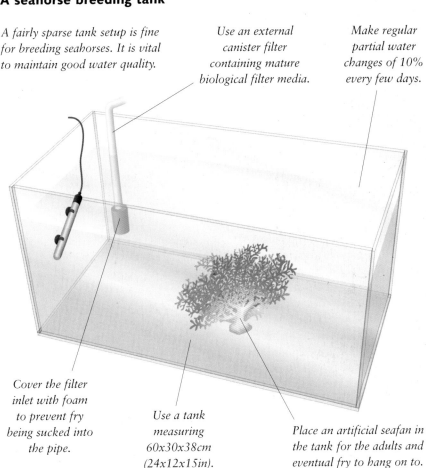

Cover the filter inlet with foam to prevent fry being sucked into the pipe.

Use a tank measuring 60x30x38cm (24x12x15in).

Place an artificial seafan in the tank for the adults and eventual fry to hang on to.

FOOD FOR ALL

Marine fishkeepers face one crucial problem. Unlike freshwater fish, which are mainly farmed commercially, almost all marine livestock is wild-caught and, therefore, completely unused to accepting prepared foods.

The feeding challenge

Obviously it is not feasible to provide the natural diet of reef-crunchers such as this parrotfish. The challenge is to provide a suitable replacement food.

Most freshwater fishkeepers can maintain healthy fish using only a staple flake food, along with, perhaps, an occasional feed of frozen food. Marine livestock offered for sale has often just arrived in an aquarium for the first time, having been shipped halfway around the world. The marine fish finds itself in a confined space, in conditions often very different from those it has lived in all its life. The stress alone can cause some marine fishes to starve in an aquarium, and most species are reluctant to accept artificial-looking flake or pellet foods, at least initially. As in all natural environments, marine fish occupy a habitat where every living organism forms part of a food chain. A small fish may eat crustaceans that may, in turn, eat algae. The small fish may be eaten by a larger fish, and so on. It is not only important to understand the obvious effects of the food chain when assessing the dietary requirements of marine fish. For example, a fish that eats algae in the wild could be fed green foods or algae, artificially grown in an aquarium. But what if, when eating the algae on the reef, the fish is also inadvertently picking up small invertebrates and crustaceans, also feeding from the algae? These tiny creatures may make up a vital part of the diet, and replacements must be found for them in an aquarium if the fish is to flourish. Small differences in diet can have major effects on the well-being of some species of marine fish. It is, therefore, essential to consider all the dietary requirements of a prospective

Below: Species such as the coral trout (Cephalopholis miniatus) *naturally prey on smaller fish. In the aquarium, their diet can be satisfied by offering lancefish.*

aquarium fish before buying it. If you cannot meet them, the fish is best left in the wild.

Marine fish fall into two main categories that describe how and where they feed. Once you understand which group your prospective purchase fits into, you can try to replicate the conditions.

Open water feeders
Open water fish are almost always bold-feeding, sometimes aggressive species that either patrol the seabed in search of a meal or look for food in the midwater regions of the ocean. They are often piscivores, meaning that they feed on smaller fish. The very fact that they feed in open water means that they are unlikely to include corals as a major part of their diet, but may not be safely housed with smaller fishes and invertebrates such as shrimps.

Coral reef feeders

Species in this category are found in and around the coral reef. They may graze on algae or pick at coral heads. Reef-feeders may also devour small fish and invertebrates that in turn feed on smaller reef-dwelling life. It is the reef-feeding group of fishes that contains many of the species that find it hard or impossible to adapt successfully to life in captivity. Reef-feeders that are extremely difficult to maintain include the regal angelfish *(Pygoplites diacanthus)*, whose diet consists mainly of sponges, and Meyer's butterflyfish *(Chaetodon meyeri)*, which thrives on specific types of live coral polyps. A great deal of detailed information is available on the feeding requirements of certain species, and you should do some careful research before making an expensive purchase that may quickly become emaciated and then die in the aquarium.

As well as being specialist feeders, coral reef fish may also be extremely shy. If housed with boisterous species, they may fail to receive sufficient food to survive for long. Fish such as blennies and gobies often require bolt-holes and areas of sand to burrow into, in order to feel confident enough to take regular feeds. Specialist feeders, such as the longnosed butterflyfish *(Forcipiger longirostris)*, which accepts only small foods that will fit into its snoutlike mouth, and which is used to picking delicately amongst coral heads, will starve if only offered pellets or large meaty foods. Similarly, many species graze continually and require a high algae content in their diet. Angelfish and surgeonfish require a constant supply of green foods to remain healthy.

Ease of feeding in the aquarium

Easy
Basses
Blennies
Clownfish
Damsels
Surgeons/tangs (certain species)
Triggers
Wrasses

Reasonably easy once feeding
Angelfish (certain species)
Butterflyfishes (certain species)
Eels
Gobies
Jawfish
Lionfish

Difficult to maintain
Angelfish (certain species)
Butterflyfishes (certain species)
Seahorses
Pipefish
Surgeons/tangs (certain species)

Nocturnal feeders

In addition to these two main groups, it is worth noting that some species are nocturnal feeders, and may require feeding after the lights have been turned off in the aquarium. Using a blue fluorescent tube as part of the lighting setup, in

order to watch the nocturnal characteristics of fish such as moray eels, can provide a fascinating insight into their behaviour. It might also provide a clue as to why there are sometimes fewer small fish in the aquarium in the morning than there were the previous day!

Providing a balanced diet

As with any living creature, fish require a balanced diet consisting of a complex blend of the right vitamins and minerals, fats, proteins and carbohydrates. Without the correct diet, fish will not grow properly. Deficiencies can manifest themselves as abnormal growth or disease, and in extreme cases, fish may even die. No single food contains everything a fish requires nutritionally, so a varied diet that includes the following nutrients is important.

Above: Many marine fish species, including this emperor angelfish, rely on copious amounts of green algae and tiny invertebrates for a balanced diet.

Proteins are made from combinations of amino acids, and are the basic building blocks from which body tissue is formed. In addition to using proteins to build and maintain tissue growth, fish will break down any surplus proteins available and use them to produce energy. The result of this excess protein is a toxic waste product in the form of ammonia (see page 18 for further details).

Fatty acids, more correctly known as lipids, are utilized to grow red muscle, essential for movement (see page 38). In addition, lipids play a vital role in the structure of individual cells and cell membranes.

Carbohydrates are provided in a fish's diet mainly through vegetable matter. They are made up of strings of simple sugars and are broken down in the gut to provide glucose. Glucose in turn is used for energy. Excess glucose is stored in the liver and muscles in a concentrated form called glycogen, which can be 'mobilized' for energy when required.

Vitamins are required for marine fish to remain healthy. The tables describe the vitamins provided by different foods and the possible symptoms of vitamin deficiency.

Foods for marine fishes

Just as 'man cannot live by bread alone', so marine fish cannot thrive on a diet consisting of a single food. A varied diet is important to maintain a mixed community of marine fishes successfully. As well as appreciating the requirements of particular species – algae, shellfish, live foods, etc., – you should vary the diet to prevent boredom at feeding time. Even lionfishes can get bored with a diet of dead lancefish, and may prefer shellfish for a change. Fortunately, a wide variety of quality foods is available to the hobbyist, and here we look at some of the more popular options.

Flake, granular and pellet foods

The staple diet of most tropical freshwater fish has come a long way in the last 20 years. As more research is done into the requirements of fish, essential vitamins and trace elements are continually updated and added to the food to make it more beneficial. Most manufacturers also offer marine flake foods that reflect the general requirements of marine fish. Several 'staple' marine flake foods are available that provide a balanced proportion to meet the needs of most species. However, the main problem with flake food still remains: it looks nothing like natural food, and it can be a frustrating experience trying to get aquarium fishes to recognize the benefits of a new food!

When tempting fish to accept flake food, try mixing it with other, more natural foods, such as frozen brineshrimp or mysis shrimp. Over a period of weeks, reduce the level of frozen food in the mix until the fish become used to the flake food.

As with all foods, ensure that uneaten flake food is not left in the aquarium, where it can break down and pollute the water. Feeding little

Sources of vitamins

Do not rely on a single food to keep marine fishes healthy. The following foods provide important vitamins.

Food Source	Vitamins
Algae	A, B_{12}, C, E
Crustaceans	A, B_2, B_6, D, K
Daphnia	D, K
Fish meat	B_2, B_6
Lettuce and other greens	A, C, B_2, B_6, B_{12}, C, E, K
Mussels	B_2, B_6, B_{12}
Shrimp	D, K

Possible symptoms of vitamin deficiency

If fish are not provided with a balanced diet, they can become ill and may eventually die. Below are some symptoms that may result from a lack of various vitamins. If these symptoms appear, examine diet and water quality as possible causes.

Vitamin	Symptom of deficiency
A	Loss of appetite, eye and gill problems, loss of weight and slow growth.
B1	Muscular wasting, poor growth, loss of balance.
B2	Eye problems such as a cloudy or bloody appearance. Poor growth and anaemia.
B6	Loss of appetite, excessive body fluid, bloating, fits.
B12	Anaemia, poor growth.
C	Reduced vividness of colour, eye diseases, deformed growth.

Flake and granular foods

Left: When feeding flake food, it is safer to offer only small amounts. Excess feeding will lead to an unnecessary strain on the biological filtration system.

Brineshrimp in flake form. Initially, you may need to mix it with live or frozen brineshrimp to tempt the fish.

High-quality mixed flake formulations contain many of the vitamins and proteins required by the majority of marine fish.

Fast-sinking granular foods can be an effective way of ensuring that bottom-feeding fish receive an ample food supply.

61

and often is far better than adding one large handful of food each day.

Granular and pellet foods are also much improved and the best now contain proteins that are easily broken down by fish and turned into growth matter. Most pellet and granular foods sink slowly through the water, allowing fish at all levels to feed. To encourage fish to accept these foods, introduce them slowly, in conjunction with live or frozen foods, as described for flake food.

Fresh meat and fish

It seems like common sense to assume that if a fish eats crabs in the wild, it would be a good idea to offer it fresh crab meat in captivity to replicate its natural dietary requirements. Indeed, this may not be a bad idea, but feeding fish regularly on fresh meat and fish can be inconvenient and you run the risk of introducing disease into the aquarium. Certainly, it is never a good idea to collect your own shellfish and invertebrates from the local shore to feed to aquarium fish. Generally, a far better option is to use some of the many prepared frozen foods now available.

Frozen foods

Specially prepared frozen foods are now available to suit the needs of most marine species. Brineshrimp, mysis, mussel, cockle and even whole silverside fish are usually sold in conveniently sized packs, with small blister cubes for ease of feeding. There have been some important

Frozen foods

Krill, a nutritious food, ideal for larger fish.

Food is available frozen in slabs and sealed in packs.

Brineshrimp, a staple food.

Whole fish for larger fishes.

A mixed diet ideal for most species.

advances in the methods used to produce frozen foods. At one time, wild-caught foods, such as brineshrimp, were merely frozen slowly in water and packed into cubes. However, modern methods, such as gamma irradiation and cryogenic freezing, have greatly reduced the chance of introducing disease into the aquarium, while also ensuring that many of the vitamins in the food are retained, thereby improving their nutritional value.

An even more recent advance in frozen fish food production is cryogenic freezing. In this method, the food is flash-frozen in a matter of seconds, which not only means that it retains all its essential vitamins and trace elements, but also prevents it from being split apart by ice crystals. When foods are frozen slowly, the water content in them begins to freeze and expand. The ice can then become too large for the body of, say, a brineshrimp and causes it to split open. This results not only in messier feeding and more wastage but, crucially for finicky

Above: A colourful firefish (Nemateleotris magnifica) *feeding on thawed-out frozen shrimp. Brineshrimp is accepted by most marine fish. It is also available enriched with spirulina or Omega-3, believed to aid growth and disease-resistance.*

feeders, in something that does not resemble a living source of food. The flash-freezing method incorporated in cryogenic production ensures that the water in the food does not have time to expand, so the food remains whole. To ensure that the food is pathogen-free, it is first laboratory tested and can be safely stored in a domestic freezer without fear of transmitting disease into food intended for human consumption.

Enhanced foods
Brineshrimp, the most commonly fed type of food, is often available in a variety of 'enriched' formulas that enhance its natural benefits. Two particularly successful types of enrichment are the addition of spirulina algae and of Omega-3 fatty acids.

Spirulina is a naturally occurring algae that is not only high in vitamins and carotenoids, but is also reported to increase resistance to stress and disease.

Omega-3 fatty acids contain substances that aid growth and promote disease-resistance. Recent tests indicate that fish fed with foods containing Omega-3 show increased coloration and a higher resistance to disease when compared with fish fed on normal brineshrimp alone.

Food enhancers work best when fed to live brineshrimp. These are then cryogenically frozen, with their intestinal tract full of the fatty acids and algae that they have been given.

Freeze-dried foods

Another popular and convenient way of feeding marine fishes is with freeze-dried foods. Larger species, in particular, appreciate cubes of mysis shrimp and krill, although it is a good idea to soak the food first. This ensures that it is not eaten as a dry lump by a greedy fish, which can cause digestive problems.

Live foods

Marine fishes always relish live foods, and sometimes they are the only way to tempt a recent addition to feed. Although marine fish will accept almost any type of live food commonly fed to freshwater fish, it is best to avoid tubifex worms, as they tend to be a fairly messy food. Ensure that any live food is well washed in fresh water before use.

Most fish will greedily accept live brineshrimp *(Artemia salina)*. These small shrimps are an excellent

Below: Daphnia is more commonly fed to freshwater fish. These small water fleas can be easily harvested and are available from most aquatic shops.

Gamma irradiation

Gamma irradiation is a method by which food potentially containing harmful micro-organisms, can be made safe for fish to consume. Gamma rays are a form of electromagnetic energy, similar to microwaves. Whereas microwaves have sufficient energy to move molecules and thus create heat, gamma radiation has more energy and can therefore discharge electrons. The resultant 'freeing' of electrons from atoms, known as ionisation, makes them available as part of a chemical reaction which can disrupt DNA. This is the fundamental mechanism by which micro-organisms are killed, thus preventing disease passing from frozen food to the fish.

Freeze-dried foods

River shrimp can be fed to medium-sized fish such as triggerfish.

Although cubed foods such as brineshrimp are less messy to use, they look less natural and may not tempt shy feeders.

Krill are greedily accepted by lionfish and groupers.

nutritious, safe food and easy to cultivate at home, either using a complete kit from your local aquatic specialist or by making a simple hatchery and buying some eggs.

Brineshrimp eggs are collected from the salt lakes of Utah and San Francisco. They are washed clean of sand and other matter, dried and packed in airtight containers. If kept in cool, airtight conditions, they can last over five years without any drop in the hatch rate.

Cultivating brineshrimp

Growing your own brineshrimp is not difficult or expensive, and can be a rewarding way to feed your fish. Brineshrimp kits are available from aquatic shops to make the whole growing process easier, but making your own hatchery is not difficult. Follow the simple steps on page 66 to start your own live food supply.

When you feed the newly hatched brineshrimp to your fish, it is vital that you do not also introduce the

Below: *Feeding live brineshrimp is an ideal way of encouraging shy fish to feed. Set up your own hatchery to be sure of a regular supply of this valuable food.*

eggshells into the tank. They are hard and often sharp and indigestible, and can harm small fish. Separating the orange-coloured brineshrimp from their shells is not difficult. Simply turn off the air supply and within a few minutes the empty shells will rise to the water surface and can be removed. Once hatched, the tiny

Hatching brineshrimp eggs

1 You will need the following equipment: brineshrimp eggs, two or three empty clear plastic bottles, a small airpump with airline, some marine salt (as used in your aquarium) and a fine net.

Use aquarium salt and not table salt.

2 In one of the bottles, mix one litre of water with two heaped teaspoons of marine salt. Add a small pinch of brineshrimp eggs. Adding too many eggs will not increase the 'harvest'; excessive newly hatched brineshrimp will simply die quickly, polluting the water. Drop in the airline attached to the airpump and switch it on. The bubbles will circulate the eggs.

Use only a small quantity of the tiny eggs at a time.

Airline

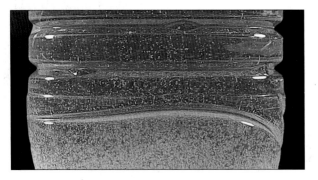

3 Stand the bottle in a dark place and keep the water at 21-24°C (70-75°F). Depending on the temperature, the eggs should hatch in 24-48 hours.

brineshrimp will survive off their yolk sack for the first 24 hours.

Most fish will benefit from feeding on larger artemia, so the shrimps will need feeding regularly with a liquid fry food until they reach the required size (which usually takes two to three days). After this, they can be netted from the bottle, rinsed in fresh water and added to the aquarium.

Vegetables

Vegetable matter, usually in the form of algae, represents an essential part of the diet for a wide variety of marine fishes. In an aquarium, it is almost impossible to maintain a sustainable level of the right algae to meet the fishes' requirements. It is therefore important to replace natural algae as a source of food, and this can be done in a variety of ways.

The easiest way of providing a vegetable diet is to offer lettuce or spinach leaves. Scald them first with boiling water to soften the leaves. Securing them in a lettuce clip with a sucker (available from aquatic shops)

ensures that the leaf is held down for the fish to feed on. A shoal of tangs or a large angelfish can devour almost a whole lettuce every day. Remove and discard any leaves that remain in the tank after 24 hours so that they do not break up and pollute the aquarium or block filters.

Alternatively, establish an algae tank. Place a small aquarium near a window and fill it with saltwater. Add some rocks or artificial corals. Within a few days they will become covered in algae and can be introduced into the main aquarium. When they have been picked clean, put them back into the algae tank for another coating. Working this way, it is easy to maintain a continuous supply of algae.

Below: Fish such as the regal tang (Paracanthurus hepatus) *require an almost constant supply of green foods, such as lettuce, spinach and algae.*

Above: To prevent green foods becoming stuck in filter inlets, secure them to the aquarium glass using a sucker and clip.

KEEPING MARINE FISH

Much of the equipment used to set up a marine aquarium is the same as that used in a freshwater tank. But because marine fish have such exacting water quality requirements, you will need extra equipment to meet these demands.

Mission accomplished

Every marine fishkeeper's dream – a stable, healthy aquarium, brimming with a display of multicoloured corals and dazzling fish.

One of the key elements in establishing a successful marine aquarium is planning. In this chapter we look at the vital decisions you will need to make and examine some of the equipment required to set up an aquarium that will successfully sustain marine fishes and, possibly, invertebrates in captivity.

Invertebrate reef tank, or fish only?
Before embarking on any equipment and livestock purchases, you will have to answer this crucial question. Bear in mind that the inclusion of

invertebrates in the aquarium will inevitably lead to changes in lighting and, possibly, filtration. Testing the water for elements such as calcium and phosphate, plus carrying out the essential tests for fish-only aquariums (pH, alkalinity, nitrite and nitrate, see page 20) becomes far more important. Furthermore, many fish

A microcosm of marine life

Above: Placing a glass box of water that represents your display aquarium over a real coral reef emphasises that it provides a tiny fraction of the environment available to these creatures in the wild. A simple image to help you appreciate the needs of marine fish and invertebrates.

are not invertebrate-compatible, as corals make up the diets of many species in the wild. It is true to say that the reef aquarium comes closest to matching the beauty of a successful reef microcosm, but invertebrates are not for the beginner.

Selecting a tank

The tank itself, the heaters, filters and light starter units are common to both freshwater and marine fishkeeping. Always remember that the majority of freshwater fishes are captive-bred and accustomed to a slightly lower level of water quality than their wild-caught relatives from the oceans, where the water conditions rarely change.

Always choose the largest possible aquarium. The stocking levels for marine aquariums are far lower than those recommended for freshwater fish, so a small tank will only support very few fish. In addition, the more water it can hold, the less tendency there will be for the water parameters to alter rapidly. For example, a 45-litre aquarium will heat up far more quickly in summer than a 360-litre aquarium. A good size is about 170 litres, equivalent to a tank measuring 100x38x45cm (39x15x18in). Later in this section, on pages 95-103, we look at a number of different marine aquarium setups, some with smaller tanks than this 'ideal' size.

Although they may look attractive, try to avoid odd-shaped aquariums, as they can be difficult to clean and 'dead' spots may be created in the water flow, where excess food and detritus collect, causing water quality problems. Instead, choose a rectangular all-glass or acrylic aquarium. Not only is saltwater corrosive, but rust is highly toxic to saltwater fishes, so make sure that there is no exposed metal in or around the aquarium that could come into contact with the saltwater.

Aquarium decor
There are many ways to decorate a marine aquarium, using tufa and ocean rock as a base for live rock in a reef aquarium, or artificial corals and algae in a fish-only system. One form of decor that is now considered unacceptable is the inclusion of dead coral. Although it was once commonly used, we have now learned enough about conservation to realize that the practice is not one that hobbyists should encourage.

Today, you can buy some extremely realistic imitation corals made of resin. These can be used in aquariums with fish that would normally devour corals, or even blended into reef aquariums to replace corals that may be impossible to maintain for any length of time.

The substrate
Choosing substrate for the marine aquarium used to be a simple affair; the choice was either coral sand or, for aquariums using old-fashioned undergravel filtration, a mixture of calcium-rich gravel or coral gravel with a coral sand top layer. Now that undergravel filters have been superseded, there is far more flexibility in the choice of substrate.

New substrates include 'live' sand, which is used in a new wave of 'natural' systems, where the aim is to create a truly self-sufficient mini-reef. Live sand aquariums actually use the substrate as a form of biological filter media. Aragonite sand, high in dissolvable calcium carbonate, has also become extremely popular due to its beneficial calcium-emitting properties that help to maintain high pH value necessary in marine systems (see page 93.)

Opinions vary as to the depth of substrate required and there is no single hard and fast rule. Some people prefer a light dusting of sand on the base of the aquarium, while others recommend a reasonable depth. The answer is to think about what the aquarium inhabitants are used to. For example, blennies and jawfishes rely on burrowing in the

Although it looks garish out of water, this simulated tree coral will soon lose its harsh appearance and add colour and interest to any display.

Above: Models of corals moulded in resin are incredibly lifelike and will soon take on the patina of realism as they become covered in algae and detritus in a marine aquarium. They are the only choice if we are to conserve the real thing in the wild.

This synthetic seafan looks surprisingly realistic, and its elegant sweeping form will contrast well with more upright shapes.

wild. Introducing them into an aquarium with little substrate does not show much understanding of their requirements. Similarly, if the aquarium does not contain creatures that constantly stir up the sand, thus preventing it from compacting and becoming dangerously anaerobic, there is little point using more than a thin layer of substrate. Appreciating the fishes' requirements and trying to meet them where possible will increase your chances of maintaining a successful aquarium.

Heating and cooling the aquarium
Using combined heater/thermostat units is perfectly adequate for heating the marine aquarium. It is far better to use two or three lower-powered units than one large one, because in the event of a failure, there is less

Below: Flash photographs taken on a reef demonstrate very clearly that light intensity falls away rapidly with distance from the light source. The same is true of sunlight as it penetrates from above.

chance of the aquarium quickly cooling or overheating.

If you keep large fish, such as moray eels or groupers, surround the heaters with a plastic mesh to prevent them being broken.

It may be necessary to prevent the aquarium overheating, especially if hot metal-halide lamps are being used or during warm summer weather. In an emergency, sealed packs of ice can be placed in the aquarium to prevent temperatures reaching critical levels, but this is obviously only a very short-term solution. If overheating is a regular problem, consider investing in an aquarium chiller.

Lighting
Not surprisingly, sunlight is more intense on a coral reef than over a tropical jungle river, where vegetation and debris dredged up in the water flow filter out much of the light. It therefore follows that the lighting requirements of an anemone or leather coral are very different from

The real colours of white light

A rainbow reminds us that white light is made up of a spectrum of colours. They are produced by different wavelengths; violet is short, red is long.

Right: *Various wavelengths of light penetrate to different depths in the sea. Blue light can reach depths of over 250m (820ft), while red light fades at about 10m (33ft). Ultra-violet light (invisible to us) can reach 100m (330ft).*

Above: *Shining a beam of white light into a glass prism produces a very clear spectrum of colours, from violet, through blue, green, yellow to red. The prism literally 'splits' the beam to reveal the colours that make it up.*

those of an Amazonian discus fish or an Asian *Aponogeton* plant.

Lighting in a fish-only aquarium is really down to personal taste. Two fluorescent tubes will usually suffice, with perhaps a third, blue lamp for night viewing. However, if there are invertebrates in the tank as well, lighting becomes far more important. Many corals, anemones and molluscs rely on algae known as zooxanthellae for food. As well as good water quality, the main requirement of zooxanthellae and macro algaes, such as caulerpa, is high intensity light at

the correct wavelength. In fish-only systems with relatively low light intensities, zooxanthellae will not grow. In a reef aquarium, the correct lighting is therefore of paramount importance and this usually means using metal-halide lamps.

There are two key elements that together contribute to the suitability of a particular tube or lamp for a given marine aquarium setup. Understanding these factors will help you to choose the best lighting system for a fish-only tank or a reef aquarium containing invertebrates.

73

How bright is a light?

Brightness, or light intensity, of a lamp is normally quoted in lumens. However, naturalists taking readings will quote the brightness in lux – the number of lumens falling onto each square metre of surface.

Typical readings vary with the time of day and water depth. Those taken at a depth of 1m (39in) on an Indonesian reef, for example, range from 2,800 lux in the morning to 26,000 lux at midday.

Sunlight over a reef

From an aquarist's point of view, the most relevant average recorded is 20,000 lux at a depth of 10-15m (33-50ft).

Metal-halide lamps

A 150-watt metal halide lamp produces 10,000 lumens.

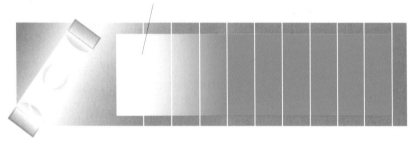

Fluorescent tubes

A 25-watt white triphosphor tube produces about 1,600 lumens.

Light intensity

There is a common misconception that the intensity of aquarium lighting is measured in watts, whereas in fact wattage is the amount of power required to make a lamp work and is standard amongst most fluorescent tubes. For example, a 60cm (24in) tube is usually 18-20 watts, a 120cm (48in) tube is usually 36-40 watts, and so on.

So if the power into a lamp is measured in watts, how do we refer to the intensity, or brightness, of a light source? The answer is in 'lumens', which are measured with a lumen meter. (You may also see light intensity quoted in terms of lux, see the panel opposite for more details.)

The intensity of a lamp is usually indicated on the packaging. Most fluorescent tubes rarely exceed 5,000-6,000 lumens, and some are far lower. On the other hand, metal-halide lamps commonly emit in excess of 10,000 lumens, so it is easy to see that you would need many fluorescent tubes to replicate a three-lamp metal-halide unit.

Light intensity also depends on the efficiency of the lamp and it is difficult to achieve high levels of light intensity with fluorescent tubes. This is especially true in deeper aquariums, where the light from most tubes fades very quickly. However bright any type of lamp may be, if it cannot penetrate through the upper water layers of an aquarium and provide the correct intensity for reef animals it is obviously of little use in a reef aquarium. A lux meter can measure whether clams, corals and other light-sensitive invertebrates are receiving the correct intensity of light, giving a reading of the light intensity at a particular point in the aquarium. If you buy a good-quality aquarium tube or lamp, the hard work will have been done for you by the manufacturer.

Another factor to bear in mind is that without sufficiently high light intensity, the aquarium may attract low-light algae, such as dark green and red varieties, that can smother corals and inhibit the growth of zooxanthellae. Furthermore, not only do you need enough light output, it must also be of the correct 'colour'.

Colour temperature

Any type of lamp, whether metal-halide or fluorescent, appears to give off light in a particular colour. In fact, the colour we perceive is made up of many different colours, each with their own spectral wavelengths. This is called the 'colour temperature' of the lamp and is measured in degrees Kelvin (°K). The higher the Kelvin rating, the more white and 'cool' the light appears. A low Kelvin rating produces a 'warm' appearance, usually predominantly red or yellow, but why should this be and why is it vital to understand?

As we see in a rainbow, light is made up of a spectrum of colours ranging from violet to red. Seawater is an efficient light filter, and different colours are filtered out at different depths. The first to go is red light, which penetrates only the very upper layers of the reef. This is followed by

What is colour temperature?

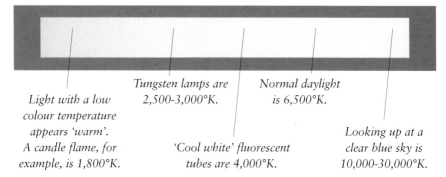

Light with a low colour temperature appears 'warm'. A candle flame, for example, is 1,800°K.

Tungsten lamps are 2,500-3,000°K.

'Cool white' fluorescent tubes are 4,000°K.

Normal daylight is 6,500°K.

Looking up at a clear blue sky is 10,000-30,000°K.

orange and yellow, both of which are also filtered out in the upper layers of the water. The most penetrative light colours are green and blue. This is why many fish that appear bright red in an aquarium, and are easy prey in shallow water, are actually rendered almost black in deeper water, as anyone who has dived off of a reef will have noticed. For example, a fire shrimp that is bought for its vivid red coloration in the aquarium, actually blends into the dark background in its natural environment.

The output of the various wavelengths of light (and therefore the strength of light in the different colour 'bands') produced by a lamp is also referred to as its spectral power distribution. You will usually see coloured graphs and diagrams on lamp packaging to reflect this.

Fluorescent lighting
The fishkeeping hobby has come a long way since the early days, when tungsten (incandescent) lighting was the norm. The first fluorescent lamps were not designed with the fishkeeper

in mind; more often than not they originated from office lighting or, as in the case of Gro-Lux tubes, from the horticulture industry.

The first major breakthrough in fluorescent lighting for aquariums came with the advent of the triphosphor lamp, which concentrates its light output in the key areas of the spectrum essential for invertebrate and macro algae growth. The spectral distribution of the lamp allows for the fact that various colours are filtered out at varying rates in seawater and compensates accordingly.

Furthermore, the lamp retains its spectral qualities until the end of its life. This is particularly important if you are using fluorescents for invertebrate aquariums, as most lamps lose part of their spectrum over a short period of time, while still emitting light. To the human eye they do not appear to have changed at all, but the deteriorating health of any corals in the aquarium often indicates a reduction in the effectiveness of the lamp.

Simulating natural light

Some aquarium lights appear bright, but it is important to remember that intensity falls rapidly with increasing distance from the light source. For example, each 1cm (0.4in) increase in distance from the lamp is equivalent to a 1m (39in) depth increase in the sea.

__Right:__ Sunlight appears to 'dapple' the water and corals on a reef. This effect can be recreated with the right lighting.

Sunlight over a reef

Normal daylight measured at the water surface has a colour temperature of about 6,500°K.

1,000°K   12,000°K

Metal-halide lamps

These can produce light with a colour temperature of 10,000°K and even higher.

Fluorescent tubes

A white triphosphor fluorescent tube produces light with a colour temperature of about 9,500°K.

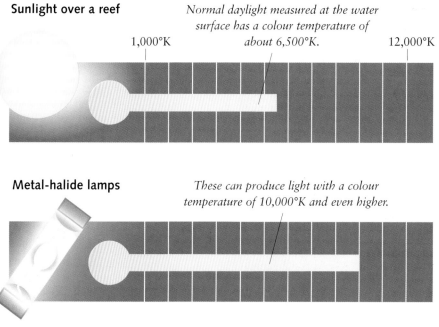

Spectral power distribution

Light is made up of many wavelengths and the balance of these produced by a light source affects its overall 'colour'. It is possible to measure which wavelengths are present and at what strengths. This is called its spectral power distribution. The graphs shown below compare the output of three light sources set against the sun's complete spectrum. Wavelengths are in nanometres (nm) – billionths of a metre.

White triphosphor fluorescent tube

These curves show that this type of lamp produces light at a wide range of wavelengths, providing bright illumination for all creatures in the aquarium. (The vertical scale reflects comparative output.)

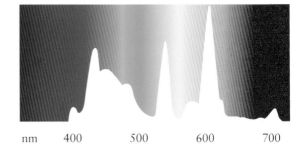

Metal-halide lamp

In common with the lamp above, this has a wide output with high levels at 400-480 nm (good for zooxanthellae) and 550 nm (to simulate sunlight). The volume of the curves here indicates a bright lamp.

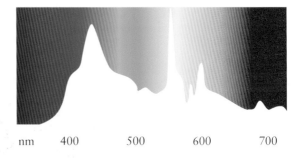

Blue actinic 03 fluorescent tube

This tube is 'strong' in the blue area of the spectrum, especially in the so-called 'actinic' range peaking at 420nm, which is vital for zooxanthellae to thrive. It also supplies some UV for a fluorescent effect.

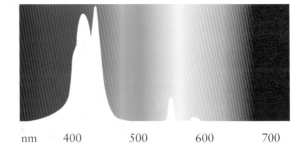

In addition to using triphosphor tubes, many aquarists use blue ones designed specifically for night viewing. Actinic blue tubes (which may be more expensive) produce ultraviolet light, essential to many types of invertebrate, as well as an attractive blue colour for night viewing. When selecting actinic tubes, be sure to buy the 03 type, which gives off a more suitable light wavelength than the similar 05 actinic tube.

The efficiency of fluorescent tubes can be greatly enhanced by using polished aluminium reflectors in the hood of the aquarium. They reflect light from the rear and top of the aquarium lid back towards the tank, increasing the effectiveness of a light by up to 50%.

Metal-halide lighting

There have been significant advances in our understanding of the light intensities and colour spectrums required by corals, and it is widely accepted now that metal-halide lamps are essential in order to maintain many coral species.

Unlike fluorescent tubes, metal-halide lamps offer a range of high-intensity outputs with hardly any size difference. The most common halide lamps are 150 watts and 250 watts, although 400 watt lamps are now available for very deep aquariums.

In addition to the high-intensity output they afford, metal-halide lamps are now available at Kelvin temperatures far better suited to the reef aquarium than used to be the case. It is now common practice to use lighting with a temperature of between 10,000 and 13,000°K. These high-Kelvin lamps create a beautiful rippling effect in the aquarium and greatly enhance the appearance of the inhabitants, as well as supplying the correct light needs for zooxanthellae to flourish.

Metal-halide lamps are usually suspended from the ceiling or a wall bracket, at least of 30cm (12in) from the surface of the aquarium, as they give off a tremendous amount of

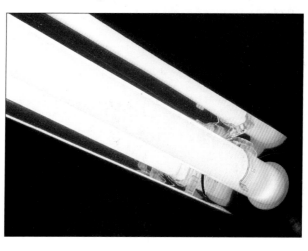

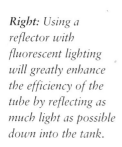

Right: Using a reflector with fluorescent lighting will greatly enhance the efficiency of the tube by reflecting as much light as possible down into the tank.

heat. The other disadvantage is their high cost, although the price of lamps and units is falling all the time.

Before you decide to keep hard corals, clams and other invertebrates that require high light levels, assess whether you are prepared to invest in the correct lighting. If the answer is 'no' then consider keeping a fish-only aquarium until funds are available to buy metal-halides. Never buy delicate corals without having the correct lighting in place to maintain them and allow them to grow.

The photoperiod

The final piece in the lighting jigsaw is the length of time the lighting is left on, known as the 'photoperiod'. There are no hard and fast rules about this, as every aquarium differs slightly in its requirements. Once again, the best way is to learn from nature and try to replicate life on the reef in your aquarium.

Around the equator, the period of sunlight is about 12 hours each day, whereas in tropical latitudes (up to about 20° north and south of the Equator), full sunlight is only experienced between about 9am to 3pm (i.e. six hours). As a starting point, if you are using fluorescent tubes, try setting your lighting period to about 12 hours. A blue lamp or one of the less bright lamps should

Below: To create a complete lighting system, you will need a variety of lighting types. This hanging unit combines white and blue actinic fluorescent tubes and a high-intensity metal-halide lamp.

come on one to two hours before the main lighting and go off one to two hours after it has been turned off. This will create a rudimentary feeling of dusk and dawn and avoids stressing nervous fish.

If you are using metal-halide lamps, try starting with a photoperiod of about eight hours, again with blue lamps that come on before the main lights and remain on after the halides have been turned off for the day.

The latest and most sophisticated artificial lighting combines metal-halide with fluorescent lighting units. It includes a programmable timer and a special 'moonlight' lamp that matches the cycle of the moon!

Protein skimmers

Most fishkeepers consider protein skimmers to be essential for the long-term success of a marine aquarium, but what do they do and how do they work?

Originally designed for the sewage treatment industry, protein skimmers, or foam fractionizers as they are sometimes called, remove harmful organic substances from the aquarium before they can cause the water quality to deteriorate.

A protein skimmer works on the principle that dissolved matter, including bacteria and plankton, as well as organic material resulting from fish waste and food, will adhere by surface tension to the outer layer of air bubbles. The rising column of air bubbles reaches the top of the skimmer's 'reaction chamber', where it falls away, leaving the protein

waste to collect at the top of the skimmer. This protein manifests itself as a thick, yellowish green, smelly liquid. Anyone who doubts the efficacy of a skimmer need look no further than a marine aquarium with a protein skimmer in operation. The oozing liquid waste that is removed from the collection cup would otherwise have to be dealt with elsewhere in the aquarium's filtration system or would remain in the water as harmful organic waste.

Contact time

Certain factors play an important role in the efficiency of a protein skimmer. One of them is contact time, the period during which air and water are mixed together in the skimmer chamber. The longer this period is, the more effective the skimmer becomes. Early skimmers consisted of a single vertical tube, where air and water were only in contact for as long as they took to rise up the tube. This meant that to skim a large aquarium effectively, huge skimmers were required to ensure a sufficient contact time. Recent advances in protein skimmer technology have led to the introduction of the Berlin-type skimmer, a patented method that uses a triple-pass method of mixing air and water.

Put simply, instead of the air and water passing through a single column, the triple-pass method incorporates two further contact chambers inside the outer chamber. This provides a much greater contact time in a compact skimmer.

Types of protein skimmer

Protein skimmers are available in three main forms, and as this is one of the most important pieces of equipment for a marine aquarium, it is worth investing in the best skimmer you can afford.

Air-operated protein skimmers are mounted inside the aquarium or sump and are generally better suited to smaller aquariums. In air-operated skimmers, a limewood diffuser provides a steady stream of fine bubbles. Although significant improvements have been made in air-operated skimmers, including the advent of the triple-pass system, they remain at the budget end of the range of available equipment.

Venturi skimmers have long been the benchmark for efficient skimming in medium-sized and large aquariums,

Triple-pass protein skimmer

Foam settling chamber

An external venturi skimmer is recommended for larger aquariums. This skimmer combines an efficient venturi system with a long contact time of air and water to produce a highly effective method of removing proteins.

Square base rests against the aquarium glass and maintains the unit in vertical position.

Air intake for venturi

Water input from pump in the aquarium.

Treated water returns to the aquarium.

Anatomy of a protein skimmer

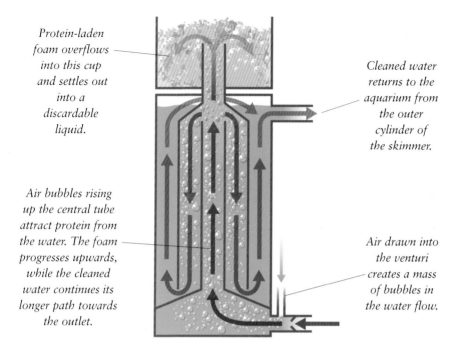

Protein-laden foam overflows into this cup and settles out into a discardable liquid.

Cleaned water returns to the aquarium from the outer cylinder of the skimmer.

Air bubbles rising up the central tube attract protein from the water. The foam progresses upwards, while the cleaned water continues its longer path towards the outlet.

Air drawn into the venturi creates a mass of bubbles in the water flow.

especially if they incorporate the 'Berlin triple-pass' method of skimming. Venturi skimmers are high-powered workhorses, operated by a water pump that takes water either from the aquarium or the sump and pushes it into the bottom of the skimmer. As water enters the skimmer, it is forced past a small, tangential opening, where air rushes in through a plastic tube. This opening is known as the venturi cone and must be built to specific designs if it is to operate efficiently. The air/water mix enters the bottom of the skimmer, where the bubbles begin to rise, initiating the whole skimming process. Venturi skimmers provide a

good air/water mix, and their effectiveness can be greatly enhanced by the addition of the triple-pass method of skimming.

Unlike air-operated skimmers, the venturi versions are usually designed to be used externally, either hanging on the side or back of the aquarium, or fitted into a below-tank sump or filter. To enhance the effectiveness of a venturi protein skimmer further, the better models can also be used with ozone (see page 90).

Turbo skimmers In the last few years, equipment manufacturers have been searching for ways to improve upon the popular venturi version of protein skimmer. Several new methods of mixing air and water have been found, the most effective being 'turbo skimming'. Put simply, a turbo skimmer is a venturi skimmer with the venturi removed or blocked off. Instead, air is injected directly into the water pump impeller housing.

To operate properly, turbo pumps use a modified 12-blade impeller that chops up the air and water into a super-fine concentrated mix. This mix is then released into the skimmer chamber, where it provides a huge surface area to which protein can adhere. Turbo skimmers, especially those using Berlin technology, have set new standards for removing protein from aquariums, demonstrating an increase of up to 40% in the efficiency of even the best conventional venturi skimmers.

The only drawback of turbo skimmers is that they cannot be used in conjunction with ozone, since the pump chamber would be destroyed by ozone's aggressive properties.

Convergent-divergent flow skimmers

The very latest skimmer design, and probably the most effective skimming method available for small and medium-sized aquariums to date, is the 'convergent-divergent' skimmer. It employs a unique method of mixing air and water, while still using the turbo method of air injection.

Filtration for marine aquariums

Although protein skimming is a type of filtration, it is important enough to be discussed in its own right. But, generally speaking, 'filtration' refers to mechanical, biological or chemical filtration, which are all used in various ways to provide marine fishes with stable, healthy water.

The filter is the life-support system of any aquarium. It not only prevents debris from remaining within the aquarium by physically removing it into a filter chamber or some other container (mechanical filtration), but also breaks down the toxic ammonia compounds released into the aquarium by fish excreta and the decay of excess food (biological filtration). If carbon or phosphate removers are used, the filter also performs chemical filtration.

You can now buy filters that are far more suited to the exacting requirements of marine fishes and invertebrates than the undergravel filters once widely used in freshwater aquariums. Here we look at some options available and consider their advantages and disadvantages.

External power filters, also known as canister filters, are fairly large filters situated externally, usually below the aquarium. Canister filters enable you to use different filter media (usually two or three) in one filter. By varying the filter media, you can incorporate all three forms of filtration – mechanical, biological and chemical.

Ideally, the filter will also have an initial prefilter sponge or foam to remove particulate waste. The foam is usually followed by a filter media with a high surface area, such as sintered glass, which is quickly populated by millions of beneficial bacteria that break down the

An external canister filter

These plastic tubes carry water to and from the aquarium.

Finally, a layer of fine polymer wool ensures that no small waste particles are allowed back into the aquarium.

Shut-off taps disconnect the filter without water spillage.

The electric water pump is housed in the top part of the filter.

Carbon removes discoloration and 'polishes' the water.

A further level of media removes fine particles.

High-surface-area media are ideal for biological filtration.

Coarse foam traps dirt particles.

Incoming water passes upwards through the filter media, packed in a plastic basket inside the canister. Maintain water flow at all times to prevent the media turning anaerobic, as would quickly happen following any failure of the power supply.

__Right:__ Cleaned water from the filter returns via a spraybar. Fit this along the back glass just beneath the water surface. Align the holes to direct water across the upper levels for gaseous exchange.

compounds causing ammonia and nitrite (see page 19). Finally, carbon may be used to remove any slight discoloration from the water and give the aquarium an extra 'sparkle'. This is known as chemical filtration.

Fluidized-bed biological filters are a relatively recent addition to the hobbyist's armoury in the battle to maintain good water quality. This type of external canister provides unsurpassed biological filtration due to its unique method of operation. Fluidized-bed filters rely on the fact that the filter medium particles in the canister are constantly circulating. This incessant movement helps prevent detritus from collecting on the surface of the highly porous medium, thus ensuring that it is able to support a maximum amount of beneficial aerobic bacteria. Additionally, fluidized-bed filters tend to convert ammonia through nitrite and into nitrate far more quickly than conventional filtration.

Sump (under-tank) filters have become an extremely popular method of filtration in recent years. Strictly speaking, they are not a single type of filter, but consist of a second aquarium underneath the main tank. This smaller aquarium houses all the filtration and heating for the main tank and is connected via an overflow from the main aquarium. A water pump, usually housed in the sump, takes water from the sump and pumps it back into the main aquarium. As the level rises in the main aquarium, water

Above: In a fluidized-bed filter the sand's moving biological bed is held in suspension (the two lines show the upper and lower levels of the medium). A valve in the unit prevents sand siphoning back into the pump if the power fails.

overflows, usually via holes drilled near the surface of the aquarium, and is carried via pipework back into the sump, where the process is repeated.

The great advantage of a sump filter is that the space afforded in most sumps allows unsightly heaters, protein skimmers and all forms of mechanical, biological and chemical filtration to be removed from view. Furthermore, the frequency of top-ups due to evaporation is reduced, as the sump provides an additional

Below: A pair of common clownfish (Amphiprion ocellaris) *nestle amongst the tentacles of their host anemone. Using efficient filtration systems in the aquarium will keep both the fish and anemone in prime condition.*

reservoir of water. An increase in the capacity of the aquarium also benefits overall water quality.

The main disadvantage of a sump filter is that it has to be planned into the aquarium setup right from the start, as it is often not practical to drill an aquarium once it has been built. However, if an aquarium is properly planned, incorporating a sump allows great flexibility.

Additional types of filtration

In addition to the filters mentioned above, there are several ancillary types of filtration. Although they are not usually essential, they can have a beneficial effect on the water quality in the aquarium and, therefore, on the health of its inhabitants.

Right: Tapwater can contain contaminants that can be removed using a reverse osmosis unit such as this. The efficiency of such units depends on the concentration of pollutants present in the water supply. Be sure to buy the correct unit for your usage.

How reverse osmosis works

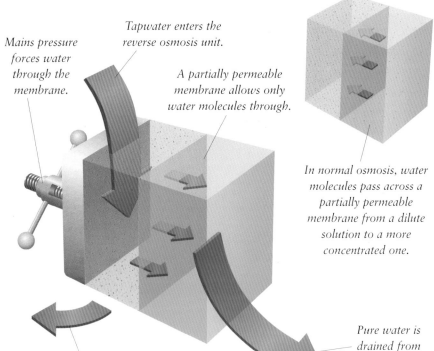

Mains pressure forces water through the membrane.

Tapwater enters the reverse osmosis unit.

A partially permeable membrane allows only water molecules through.

In normal osmosis, water molecules pass across a partially permeable membrane from a dilute solution to a more concentrated one.

Pure water is drained from the unit.

Left over water can be used on the garden.

Reverse osmosis units Thus far we have only discussed equipment required for treating water once it is in the aquarium. However, one of the easiest ways to get ahead in the quest for good water quality is to ensure that only the very best water is used in the first place. To make it safe for human consumption, tapwater contains not only chlorine, but also pesticides, nitrates, phosphates and silica, all of which are detrimental to the health of marine animals. To prevent these substances from ever entering the aquarium, you are strongly advised to use a reverse osmosis unit.

Reverse osmosis is a process that removes salts and minerals from the water, plus the toxins mentioned above, as well as some bacteria, viruses and fungal spores. The key to a reverse osmosis unit is a partially permeable membrane that allows water to pass through, but repels all the other substances. Typically, a reverse osmosis unit will have a carbon prefilter to remove chlorine from the incoming water.

An R.O. unit is usually simple to plumb into a domestic coldwater supply. The only real drawback is that typically three to four times as much 'reject' water has to be discarded for every measure of 'good' water. However, the discarded water is suitable for watering plants, as it is high in useful nutrients.

Using a good-quality salt mix will ensure that the correct trace elements and minerals are restored to the R.O. water before it is added to the tank. If you are using R.O. water for a freshwater top-up, you must use a marine buffer and trace element additive in conjunction with the water change.

Ozone The use of ozone has become more widespread in recent years, partly due to the availability of improved dosing methods and partly because it is now recognized as an extremely effective method of preventing disease outbreaks, boosting water quality and enhancing the efficiency of protein skimmers.

The natural biological cycle in an aquarium results in a build-up of ammonia from waste products in the water. Left untreated, this can rise to unhealthy levels. Ozone is an effective way of eliminating ammonia from aquariums.

Ozone (O_3) is an unstable form of oxygen with an extra oxygen atom added to the stable molecular form (O_2) It is a strong oxidizer and natural purifying agent. When correctly applied to aquarium water, ozone kills bacteria and other harmful pathogens and breaks down ammonia and other organic waste materials. One of the most visible results of using ozone as part of aquarium filtration is that the water no longer has a yellow tinge, but is crystal clear. As excessive ozone can affect the chemical composition of seawater, it is a good idea to use a combined ORP (oxidation, reduction potential) meter and ozonizer.

Ozone cannot be introduced directly into the aquarium, so it is usually injected into the venturi of a protein skimmer (see page 90). It is

Ozone and protein skimming

Froth carrying organic waste overflows into a collecting cup.

The waste can be drained from the base of the cup through this tube.

Above: Activated carbon placed in a compartment on top of the collecting cup prevents any excess ozone entering the atmosphere.

A check valve prevents water siphoning back into the ozonizer. Renew it regularly.

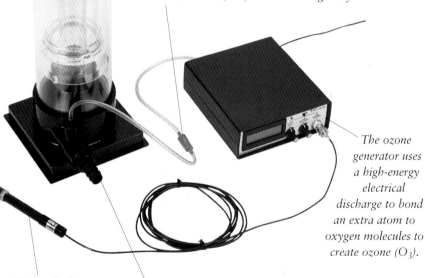

The ozone generator uses a high-energy electrical discharge to bond an extra atom to oxygen molecules to create ozone (O_3).

This probe hanging in the tank measures the redox potential of the water and regulates the amount of ozone produced by the ozonizer.

Ozone passes into the water flow through the venturi device located here.

always advisable to pass the outflowing water over activated carbon before it enters the aquarium. This will prevent harmful ozone from coming into contact with livestock.

Ultraviolet (UV) sterilizers A great deal has been written about the effectiveness of ultraviolet sterilizers in an aquarium and the best way to use them. While no-one doubts their ability to kill off algae in pond water, many marine hobbyists add a UV sterilizer to their aquarium and expect it to safeguard the fish against parasites and other diseases. This complacency often leads to heart-wrenching mass losses when diseases go unnoticed until it is too late.

The efficiency of a UV sterilizer is governed by several factors, including the cleanliness of the water, the length of time the water is in contact with the UV lamp, the age of the lamp and the cleanliness of the quartz sleeve that surrounds it.

Ultraviolet sterilization is effective against algae spores and can be effective against some bacteria and parasites. However, the UV light can only destroy what it sees, and then only if there is enough contact time between the pathogen and the light. Passing dirty water through a UV unit will reduce the effectiveness of the lamp, as the light will lose much of its power as it penetrates the dirty water. Pumping water too quickly through a UV will not allow sufficient time for the light to have an effective 'kill rate'. As an approximate guide, allow a rating of

How a UV sterilizer works

The aquarium water can be sterilized by passing it through a UV unit. The water hose connectors are translucent so that you can see the 'glow' of the UV lamp when in operation, a safety measure to make sure you do not open the unit and damage your eyesight.

Water flows though this outer glass tube.

This quartz sleeve encases the tube but allows UV light to pass through.

The fluorescent tube in the middle produces ultraviolet light with a wavelength of 253.7 nm. This UVC is harmful to living tissue.

1 watt per 5 litres of aquarium water, and ensure that the flow rate through the UV unit is no more than twice every hour. Ideally, the UV should be recirculating aquarium water that has been prefiltered via a small power filter, run separately from the aquarium's main filtration.

Nitrate and calcium control
As we have seen, understanding the water requirements of marine species – both fish and invertebrates – is a key element in maintaining a successful aquarium. By the time you have bought an aquarium and are looking for suitable livestock, you should have a rudimentary understanding of the nitrogen cycle and how to monitor and control it (see page 19). It is also vital that you

appreciate the importance of maintaining stable salinity. Those hobbyists who wish to pursue their interest a little further and progress onto either reef aquariums with highly sensitive stony corals, or fish aquariums with delicate, nitrate-intolerant species such as some butterflyfishes, will need to understand the importance of two further elements of water quality.

Nitrate control Many delicate species of fish and coral are highly intolerant of even moderate nitrate levels, and

*Below: This tropical clam (*Tridacna crocea) *forms a superb feature in a marine aquarium. It needs strong lighting for the zooxanthellae and a high calcium level to maintain its twin shells.*

in order for them to flourish, nitrate levels in the aquarium must be kept to an absolute minimum. While this can be achieved to a certain extent by regular water changes with R.O. water, nitrates have a habit of rising and additional action may be necessary. There are several nitrate reduction systems available to the hobbyist and they vary greatly in their ease of use.

The simplest way to encourage nitrate control is to maintain a reef aquarium with a high quantity of living rock, which develops its own nitrate-reducing properties over time. It is also possible to maintain nitrates at near zero levels simply by adding living rock to the sump of a fish-only system. For a 450-litre aquarium, as little as 15kg (33lb) of living rock

can be sufficient to control nitrate levels. However, this is not an instant solution, as living rock takes time to mature in the aquarium.

If a 'natural' system is not a practical solution, there are artificial methods of nitrate control. These are usually available in the form of an automated or manual nitrate-reactor. A nitrate-reactor is usually a sealed container that encourages the growth of a certain type of nitrate-reducing bacteria. These bacteria are only present in an oxygen-free environment and need feeding in order to survive. Automated nitrate-reactors can be regulated using a redox controller. A redox controller is a device that allows the ORP (oxidation reduction potential) of the aquarium to be adjusted. In simple terms, ORP measures the cleanliness of the water.

Calcium control Many reef aquariums have a high level of calcium usage, usually as a result of hard coral growth, clams and other calcareous invertebrates. If it is not possible to maintain a stable calcium level by regular water changes, it may be necessary to add extra calcium to the aquarium. There are various ways of doing this, but whatever method you choose, you must use an accurate calcium test kit.

The simplest way to add calcium is by using a liquid supplement such as calcium chloride. Just dilute the recommended dosage in saltwater and add it to the sump or pour it slowly into the aquarium. If you prefer a more scientific method of

Above: This fish-only aquarium provides generous swimming space for wimplefish (Heniochus acuminatus) and regal tangs (Paracanthurus hepatus). The decor is made from expanded polystyrene.

calcium dosing, choose a product that replaces the calcium and carbonate ions in the water. The very best of these do so in a way that allows you to measure the growth of corals by combining the results of accurate alkalinity and calcium tests, and adding the required 'Calk' mixture. Using this method it has been possible to determine that

adding 28gm (1oz) of Calk to the aquarium will build 10gm (0.4oz) of coral skeleton. This system of calcium dosing is a great

being injected into a vessel containing hydrocarbonate. The carbon dioxide causes the pH to drop, the hydrocarbonate dissolves and releases calcium into the aquarium.

Providing a natural environment
The main objective for most marine fishkeepers is to provide a habitat for their fish that is as natural as possible. The items of equipment examined earlier in this chapter vary in their degree of importance, but all are designed to serve one purpose – to help maintain a healthy marine aquarium. They are a means to an end and should not distract you from the main goal, which is to achieve and sustain a balanced environment for your livestock.

   With so many different natural habitats to try to replicate, no two aquariums need ever look the same. There is no definitive 'right' way to keep marine fish; the guide that follows is just that – a guide. The advice has proved successful, but this is by no means the only way to keep the myriad of species of marine fish available to hobbyists today.

Fish-only tanks for larger species
This type of aquarium is suited to large fish, such as wrasses, angelfishes, groupers and puffers. Species of this type are unsuited to invertebrate aquariums and require open swimming spaces combined with sturdy rockwork. You will need a tank that holds at least 450 litres. Keep the decor simple, with perhaps a central rock formation constructed from tufa or ocean rock. Make it as

improvement on the old-fashioned method of adding 'Kalkwasser', or limewater, to the aquarium. This can cause drastic changes in the pH and, if over-used, can cause complete aquarium wipeouts.

   If you prefer an automated calcium dosing system, you can buy a calcium reactor, albeit at a premium price. It relies on carbon dioxide

95

stable as possible, using a marine-safe sealant to glue the rocks together if necessary. Leave space for the fish to swim around the central formation. A thin layer of sand about 6mm (0.25in) deep is all that is required, unless you include digging or burrowing wrasses.

The filtration system should be designed for messy eaters that create a lot of waste. Mechanical filtration will have to cope with broken-off greens, such as lettuce and spinach, as well as large meaty foods such as cockle and mussel. A powerful protein skimmer is essential and an ozonizer, although not vital, would further enhance the water quality in the aquarium for nitrite-intolerant inhabitants such as angelfish.

If possible, install an external heating system that cannot be damaged by boisterous fishes. The lighting requirements are relatively undemanding; two fluorescent lamps are perfectly acceptable.

Species aquarium for eels, anglerfish, octopus and lionfish
Use an aquarium with a capacity of at least 340 litres and make sure that the rockwork is glued firmly into place. You can include rockwork to represent a reef backdrop and site it towards the back of the aquarium.

The filtration and heating should be robust enough to cope with the often messy fish that produce substantial amounts of waste. An external power filter is ideal for this

Above: The fascinating blue ribbon eel (Rhinomuraenia quaesita) *from the Pacific can be kept in aquariums. It grows to about 75cm (30in) long and may be difficult to feed. Fit a secure lid on the tank!*

Left: The tropical octopus (Octopus cyaneus) *grows to a diameter of about 30cm (12in) and is suitable for a tank with plenty of rocky caves but no fish or crustaceans. (They are potential meals!)*

type of aquarium. A tightly fitting lid is essential if you are keeping eels or octopus, as they are escape experts. Provide subdued lighting with, perhaps, one fluorescent tube and a blue light for night-time viewing. Many predatory fish such as eels are nocturnal hunters that prefer to rest during the daylight hours in a rocky cave or crevice.

Exercise extreme caution when carrying out any cleaning or general maintenance, as many fish suited to this type of aquarium will either bite or sting. Although lionfish tend only to sting if threatened, eels can be more aggressive. Their eyesight is poor, and a finger can be mistaken for an easy meal! A bite from a moray eel can be painful and liable to infection. A set of long handle prongs is ideal for feeding time.

Mixed community aquariums

For people with less space, there are many species of fish ideally suited to a smaller aquarium. However, as we have seen, maintaining good water quality is somewhat more difficult in a smaller body of water, so small does not mean basic if the aquarium is to succeed in the long term.

Ideal species for a 160-litre aquarium include blennies, gobies, clownfish, basslets and damselfish. Gobies and blennies are used to digging and burrowing, so they will

Below: This mixed community aquarium includes clownfishes, wreckfishes, damsels and chromides. The rockwork is studded with live corals and anemones, plus macro-algae such as caulerpa.

need a substrate of soft sand at least 7.5cm (3in) deep. Basslets generally require several places of refuge amongst rock formations in order to feel confident.

There are several possibilities regarding decor, depending on your taste. While most people choose to build up a vertical reef effect at the back of the aquarium, it is possible to create a very effective natural environment for many reef species by laying the rocks out horizontally over the base of the aquarium. Anyone who has been diving will know that the flat coral formations in a lagoon are teeming with life. Experiment with different layouts in the tank before adding any water and try to envisage where you might place any

artificial corals in order to give the aquarium a realistic appearance.

As with any other marine aquarium setup, it is vital to include a protein skimmer and suitable filtration. However, it is less important to mount the equipment externally, as the species suited to a small, mixed community aquarium are incapable of damaging it.

To replicate faithfully the environment from which reef-dwelling fish originate, it is essential to include some live corals and other invertebrates. This means satisfying their lighting requirements and you should be prepared either to provide metal-halide lighting or to leave certain corals where they belong. However, with careful selection, it is possible to achieve great success using only fluorescent lighting.

When selecting invertebrates for a mixed aquarium using only fluorescent lighting, look no further than soft corals, such as leather and cauliflower corals, as well as hermit crabs and shrimps. Certain types of anemone can be maintained successfully without the extra illumination provided by metal-halide lamps; the sand anemone *(Heteractis aurora)* is perhaps the most suitable. Provide additional water flow using a powerhead to replicate the constant water movement found on a reef.

The combination of small, colourful fish, along with the delicate flowing movement of corals and the ever-interesting mix of hermit crabs

and shrimps, ensures that even a relatively small marine aquarium can be extremely rewarding.

A reef aquarium

The ultimate type of aquarium for most marine hobbyists is a reef aquarium populated by an abundance of corals and macro-algae. Such aquariums often contain very few fish, as the main focus is on invertebrates. A reef aquarium is often best decorated using a base of tufa with live rock placed on top. Alternatively, glass shelves can be siliconed into the aquarium, with live rock placed on top. This method has the added advantage that valuable water space is not displaced by tufa or ocean rock.

When buying live rock, always ensure that it has been properly treated before adding it to an established aquarium. Uncured rock will give off high levels of toxic ammonia. Once it has become established, the rock will develop attractive algae, coral and sponge growths. Reef aquariums are best illuminated by metal-halide lamps, in order to provide the correct intensity and light wavelengths for the zooxanthellae required by many corals and other invertebrates to grow (see page 79).

Water quality in a reef aquarium must be of a high quality and it is fortunate that once it has become established, living rock is capable of nitrate reduction in the aquarium. Not only do hard corals require the correct lighting and good water quality, they also benefit considerably from a high water flow, provided by suitable powerheads. Furthermore, powerheads provide a flow of water

Left: This elegant soft coral (Xenia sp.) is an excellent choice for a reef aquarium. It is one of many shallow-water corals that have photosynthetic zooxanthellae in their tissues and therefore need a good source of light to sustain them.

Left: This blood shrimp (Lysmata debelius) *will bring interest and constant movement to a reef aquarium. Like many other tropical shrimps, this one will provide 'cleaning services' to any fish in the tank.*

that washes away any detritus from the surface of corals, and prevents them from rotting away.

Given the amount of equipment generally required to maintain a reef aquarium, it is a good idea to use a sump system and to house the protein skimmer, heating units, filtration and recirculation pumps outside the aquarium. The only pieces of equipment required inside the aquarium are the powerheads to provide strong water currents, which can easily be hidden amongst rocks.

Reef tanks of less than 450 litres are not recommended, especially for less experienced hobbyists, as the exacting water requirements of hard corals are extremely difficult to maintain in a small aquarium.

Left: This coral (Pseudoptergorgia acerosa) *is a gorgonian, a family that includes the flat-sided seafans. It is easy to keep, given space and good lighting.*

Overleaf: A well set up reef aquarium can provide a colourful and compelling window on the natural world beneath the surface of the tropical seas.

POPULAR MARINE FISH

The sheer variety of suitable marine fish to choose from is one of the main reasons for the hobby's popularity. Here, we take a brief overview of the most popular families of fishes, their suitability, behaviour and feeding habits.

When you come to buy your marine fish, bear in mind that within every family of fishes there are anomalies. Not all species in a particular family may be suitable for aquarium life, so use this section as a broad guide only, and when choosing fish for your aquarium, always seek the advice of your specialist aquatic dealer. Give them accurate information about the size of your aquarium and the existing inhabitants. Find out as much as possible about the fish and invertebrates you want to keep.

A painter's palette

The stunning coloration of the lipstick tang does not fade in adulthood, as it does in some marines. It needs plenty of swimming space to attain full size.

Acanthuridae – surgeons and tangs

Many of the fish in this family are eminently suited to aquarium life. Particular favourites are the lipstick tang *(Naso lituratus)*, the yellow sailfin tang *(Zebrasoma flavescens)* and the powder blue surgeonfish *(Acanthurus leucosternon).*

Surgeonfish are readily identifiable by their lateral compression, distinctive fins and the scalpel-like spines at the base of the tail, which account for their common name. These spines are used both in defence against predators, and when the fish are disputing territory on the reef.

Some surgeonfish can reach about 45cm (18in) in length, although adult fish rarely attain half this size in an aquarium. In the wild they are found in large shoals near the protection of coral reefs. This gregarious behaviour does not usually apply to aquarium specimens, which quarrel fiercely in the confines of anything but the largest tanks, so keep surgeonfish as single specimens. Occasionally, they also fight for territory with fish of similar coloration. For example, a yellow sailfin tang may become aggressive towards a lemonpeel

angelfish *(Centropyge flavissimus)*, so this is also something to consider when choosing suitable companions for surgeonfish.

Surgeons and tangs require regular feeding, and once acclimatized to aquarium life, will take a wide variety of frozen and live foods. Tangs are voracious herbivores, grazing constantly on algae found around coral reefs throughout the world. If introduced into an aquarium containing little or no algae, green foods must be made constantly available to them. Lettuce and spinach are popular; supplement these with frozen foods, such as mysis shrimp and brineshrimp.

There are few colour changes between juveniles and adults in the surgeonfish family, although one of the popular species, the Caribbean blue tang *(Acanthurus coeruleus)*, has

Right: In common with most tangs and surgeonfish, the yellow sailfin tang (Zebrasoma flavescens) *requires copious amounts of greenfood in its diet in order to remain healthy.*

105

Above: Triggers are unsuitable for invertebrate aquariums, but can make interesting inhabitants in fish-only setups. This is Balistes vetula.

yellow coloration as a juvenile that changes to a dark blue with striped fins as it enters adulthood.

Surgeons and tangs are somewhat prone to oodinium and marine whitespot parasitic infections, and although relatively hardy and long-lived, they do not tolerate poor water quality. Keep nitrate levels to a minimum and carefully check the fish in this family for whitespot before introducing them into an established aquarium. As this parasite occurs mainly when fish become stressed or weakened, it is important to provide the right conditions for aquarium specimens from the outset. Because of their tendency to contract these diseases, think carefully before

adding them to a reef aquarium, where copper-based treatments cannot be used. However, surgeons and tangs are a bright and interesting addition to a well-kept aquarium.

Balistidae – triggerfishes

This popular family of fishes has acquired its common name because of the triggerlike locking dorsal spine. The spine usually lies flat, but can be firmly locked into position if the fish feels threatened. Anyone who has tried to remove a 'locked-in' trigger from a crevice in rockwork will testify to the strength of the spine. If it remains locked, the only way to free the fish from a hand net is often to cut it out, ruining the net in the process!

Triggerfish are some of the most charismatic of all marine fish, quickly becoming hand-tame and accepting a variety of meaty frozen foods from their owners. They have a highly distinctive shape – almost like a diamond on its side – and their coloration varies greatly, from dark blue through to the psychedelic patterns of the aptly named Picasso trigger *(Rhinecanthus aculeatus)* and the highly sought-after clown trigger *(Balistoides conspicillum)*.

In the wild, triggers like nothing more than crunching on corals and are therefore entirely unsuited to invertebrate aquariums. They can also be quite destructive, with a habit of moving sand and rockwork around the aquarium. This may stem from their natural breeding behaviour, which includes digging pits in the sandy ocean floor.

Other than at breeding time, triggers are a solitary species, so keep them away from fish of the same family in an aquarium. They are territorial and can be very aggressive towards fish of all sizes. They have a

deserved reputation as a belligerent species, but when kept with other robust fish, can make ideal aquarium inhabitants, often acquiring a 'personality' all of their own.

Triggers benefit from a widely varied diet, which should include green foods as well as shrimp, cockle and other meaty foods.

Blenniidae – blennies

Blennies are another very rewarding family of fishes for the aquarium. These generally small fish spend much of their time peering out of crevices or abandoned shells and must be provided with suitable hiding spaces in order to flourish. Although most may be happily

Below: Scooter blennies (Petroscirtes temmincki) *are ideal fish for reef aquariums. They spend most of their time searching for food, 'scooting' around the bottom of the aquarium.*

Above: Psychedelic fish (Synchiropus picturatus) *spend most of their time at the bottom of the tank. Make sure they receive ample food before it is eaten by top and midwater species.*

Left: Synchiropus splendidus *is a shy species, not suited to aquariums containing active or aggressive fish. For best results, keep mandarinfish singly in a mature reef aquarium.*

accommodated with other fish, they can be territorial, especially towards their own species, so check out the behaviour of specific fish in the family before adding them to an aquarium. Some species, such as the popular scooter blenny *(Petroscirtes temmincki)*, appear to benefit from being kept in groups.

Most blennies are omnivorous and will take a wide variety of dried and frozen foods. Being generally shy bottom-feeders, make sure that food reaches them – something of a problem if particularly boisterous inhabitants share the aquarium. Blennies definitely benefit from being kept in a peaceful aquarium with invertebrates and small, non-aggressive fish.

Callionymidae – mandarins and psychedelic fish

These fish are extremely popular, but sadly, many do not flourish in aquariums. They are a family of small, bottom-dwelling fishes that survive longest in mature invertebrate aquariums with peaceful companions, such as seahorses, shrimps and corals. Their diet naturally consists of small crustaceans and parasitic copepods living in and around corals.

Mandarins and psychedelic fish can be territorial towards each other and are best kept either singly or in matched pairs. Sexing these small fish is fairly simple; the males have significantly longer dorsal fins than females and are often more vividly marked. One possible drawback to keeping these beautiful fish is that

when stressed, they appear to shed a toxic mucus that can affect their aquarium companions, although there is little firm data available to confirm this.

Chaetodontidae – butterflyfish

This family includes some of the most popular species for the marine aquarium, but before undertaking to keep them, be sure that you can provide the ideal environment for these generally demanding fish.

Butterflyfish are easy to recognize by their distinctive, laterally compressed body shape. Generally speaking, they also have a terminal mouth – like a pair of lips – and this is an indication of their preferred diet, which consists mainly of the heads and tips of soft corals and featherdusters. Other favourite foods include sponges, green foods and many of the small creatures that inhabit corals. A huge variety of species is commonly available to the hobby, but the fish vary greatly in their ability to adjust to life in an aquarium. Thankfully, we now have a far greater knowledge of their specific requirements and as a result of modern legislation, there is no longer any trade in many species that do not prosper in an aquarium. For example, Meyer's butterflyfish *(Chaetodon meyeri)*, is rarely offered for sale. Even once popular fish such as the well-known copperband butterfly *(Chelmon rostratus)* are not suitable for the average hobbyist due to their specific dietary requirements. Before buying a butterflyfish, find out what it needs

Above: *With their long extensions to the front few rays of the dorsal fin and bold pattern, wimplefish* (Heniochus acuminatus) *create a stunning visual effect in large tanks, where they can be kept in small shoals.*

Right: *Raccoon, or lunula, butterflyfish* (Chaetodon lunula) *are more suited to aquarium life than many other species in the family. They benefit from regular feeds of brineshrimp.*

Above: The delicate snout of Forcipiger longirostris *is a clue to its natural diet of coral polyps. It can be kept successfully with non-aggressive companions in fish-only aquariums of over 200 litres.*

Below: The sunburst, or Klein's, butterflyfish (Chaetodon kleini) *is one of the easiest butterflyfishes to keep. Once settled into the aquarium, it is hardy and peaceful. It will reach about 10cm (4in).*

111

in order to flourish in an aquarium and ask yourself honestly if you can provide those necessities. Modern fishkeepers accept that it is not enough for fish simply to survive for a certain time in the aquarium. Each inhabitant should be acquired in the belief that it can be kept properly and will lead a healthy life. If you are in any doubt as to the suitability of your aquarium, seek advice from a specialist aquatic retailer.

Species from this family that are more suited to aquarium life include the wimplefish *(Heniochus acuminatus)*, the sunburst butterfly *(Chaetodon kleini)* and the raccoon butterfly *(Chaetodon lunula)*, all of which will readily accept a variety of

Below: As with other species in this family, the longspined porcupinefish (Diodon holacanthus) *benefits from a mixed diet that includes shellfish, which it crunches with its powerful, fused front teeth. Keep it in a fish-only setup.*

frozen foods and usually settle quickly into an aquarium.

Generally speaking, fish from the family Chaetodontidae require reasonably large aquariums with a mixture of hiding places and areas of open water. Water quality must be excellent if these fish are to prosper, and they should be offered a wide variety of foods several times each day, as they are natural grazers.

Given their natural diet of corals and sponges, butterflyfish are totally unsuited to invertebrate aquariums. Keep them with relatively peaceful fish of the same or a smaller size.

Diodontidae – porcupinefish

Porcupinefish are similar to pufferfish in their ability to inflate themselves when threatened, and have become extremely popular aquarium fish. They are easy to distinguish from pufferfish by the spines on their bodies. The two commonest species are the longspined porcupinefish

(Diodon holacanthus) and the spiny boxfish *(Chilomycterus schoepfi)*, both of which have the typical fused front teeth of other fish in the family.

Porcupinefish benefit from a meaty diet, including mussels and shrimps. They are ideally suited to fish-only systems, as they will devour any crustaceans in the tank. They often 'rest' for long periods and are not particularly adept swimmers; rather, they propel themselves around the aquarium when food is offered. Many hobbyists like these fish because they seem to be able to recognize their owners – especially at feeding time!

Gobiidae – gobies

This is one of the largest families of marine fishes, with species inhabiting oceans all around the world. Given this variety, it is not possible to supply specific details of their requirements, but on the whole gobies are peaceful fish that become confident once established in an aquarium. Most are

bottom-dwellers that can be distinguished from the similar-looking blenny family by the sucker-type disc underneath the pelvic fins and their generally bright colours.

Make sure that food reaches the bottom of the aquarium where gobies can eat it and that larger, more aggressive feeders do not prevent these bottom-feeders from receiving ample amounts of food, including live and frozen foods.

Many fish in this family feed on parasites found on other fish and can be useful aquarium inhabitants for this reason. Their peaceful demeanour, easy care and bright coloration make them a justifiably popular aquarium addition.

Below: The sand-sifting behaviour of the Rainford's goby (Amblygobius rainfordi) *is typical of species in this family. These fish fare better in a reef tank, where the security of plenty of hiding places among the rocks will increase their confidence.*

Grammidae – grammas

Two species from this family are frequently offered for sale and they are popular choices for fish-only and reef aquariums.

The front half of the strikingly coloured royal gramma *(Gramma loreto)* is magenta, while the rear of the body and the tail are gold or yellow. This fish can be aggressive towards its own species, as well as other fish sharing its cave habitat. With a maximum size of about 8cm (3.2in) in the aquarium, the royal gramma is an ideal species for tanks of all sizes. It is particularly suited to reef tanks, where the choice of hideaways give it confidence, so that this initially shy species will venture out more regularly. Given time, it becomes a bold feeder, accepting most frozen and live foods.

The black cap gramma *(Gramma melacara)* is also highly distinctive, with a solid magenta body and, as

Below: The peaceful black cap gramma (Gramma melacara) *is a much sought-after species for reef aquariums. It adapts readily to aquarium life and feeds on most prepared foods.*

the name suggests, a black cap. Usually slightly smaller than the royal gramma, this species is somewhat less boisterous and also requires plenty of hiding places. Black cap grammas will fight with their own species, so keep single specimens. They will accept most frozen and live foods and are ideally suited to an invertebrate aquarium.

Labridae – wrasses, hogfish and tuskfish

The Labridae family is one of the largest of all aquarium fishes, encompassing a huge variety of shapes, sizes and dispositions. It includes not only wrasses, but also hogfish and tuskfish.

Particularly common species of wrasse include the clown *(Coris gaimardi)*, the African clown *(Coris formosa)*, the birdmouth *(Gomphosus caeruleus)* and the twinspot *(Coris angulata)*, all of which are fast-growing and can attain lengths of 20-30cm (8-12in). When juvenile, all these species are acceptable invertebrate aquarium inhabitants, but they quickly become destructive diggers and can cause

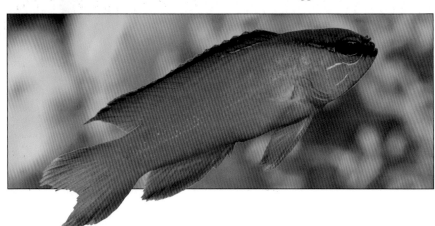

Above: The twinspot wrasse (Coris angulata) grows quickly and requires a large aquarium to attain its full size. The juveniles pictured here will turn green with yellow-edged purple fins as adults.

Below: This is a juvenile African clown wrasse (Coris formosa). As with many other marine species, it changes its appearance in adulthood, with a different pattern on the body and fins.

Above: The Cuban hogfishes (Bodianus pulchellus) *are bold feeders that will accept most foods in the aquarium. In the wild, they act as cleaner fish, removing parasites from their 'customers'.*

corals and rockwork to topple over. Given their relatively large adult size, these fish are therefore more suited to bigger aquariums, where they will benefit from a layer of sand in which to hide away.

Far better choices for a reef aquarium are smaller species including the pyjama, or sixline, wrasse *(Pseudocheilinus hexataenia)*, the dragon, or reindeer, wrasse *(Novaculichthys taeniorus)* and

banana wrasses *(Halichoeres chrysus)*. These species rarely exceed 5-6cm (2-2.4in) and are peaceful, undemanding fish to keep. In common with their larger cousins, smaller wrasses appreciate plenty of rockwork in which to hide, and a layer of sand. They will readily accept most aquarium foods.

Possibly the best known of all the species in this family is the cleaner wrasse *(Labroides dimidiatus)*, which has been the subject of many underwater documentaries, not least for its cleaning activities. In the wild, this species picks parasites off the skin of other fish and is spared being devoured by larger fish as they stand, head-down in the water, being picked clean. While the cleaner wrasse has long been a popular species, it is not really suited to captive life. Although it readily accepts a variety of frozen foods, the lack of a regular diet of parasites appears to cause the fish to waste away and its life expectancy in captivity is not long. It is better to leave the fish to their natural world, where they continue to flourish.

Hogfish are represented by two popular species, the Spanish hog *(Bodianus rufus)*, and the Cuban hog *(Bodianus pulchellus)*. They are both colourful species that are well suited to medium-sized aquariums. Like the larger wrasses, they can become somewhat belligerent towards invertebrates as they mature and are probably best suited to aquariums where they are housed with species of a similar size and disposition.

The harlequin tuskfish *(Lienardella fasciata)* from the western Pacific has always been a popular choice for hobbyists with larger fish-only aquariums due to its bright coloration and unusual appearance. Despite looking fierce on account of its prominent set of teeth, this is a peaceful, undemanding species that can quickly grow to about 30cm (12in) when fed on a diet of meaty foods, including shrimps and mussels. Keep it with fish of the same size or larger.

Microdesmidae – firefish

The firefish *(Nemateleotris magnifica)* and the purple firefish *(Nemateleotris decora)* are similar in appearance to blennies and gobies and ideal inhabitants for most aquariums. In the wild, these fish are seen in large groups, never straying far from the security of the reef, where they soon disappear if danger

Below: The colourful purple firefish (Nemateleotris decora) *is less common than* N. magnifica. *Given plenty of decor in which to hide, these pretty fish will settle well into aquarium life.*

threatens. The highly distinctive
first dorsal ray can be locked into
position to anchor the fish into a
crevice in the reef. They reach
about 7cm (2.75in) in length.

Firefish are generally peaceful,
except towards members of their
own species, with whom they will
fight if housed in confined spaces.
Keep single specimens in smaller
tanks. These fish accept most
aquarium foods and are easy to feed.

Muraenidae – moray eels
Few fish can conjure up the same
instant image as the moray eel.

*Above: A tight-fitting aquarium lid and
a set of tongs are essential items of
equipment when keeping eels such as
this snowflake moray* (Echnida nebulosa).

Although often depicted as a dark,
menacing species more than 2m (6ft)
long, there are in fact many species in
this varied family.

Most species of moray eel are
nocturnal predators that rarely leave
their rocky hideaways. All have very
sharp teeth that can inflict painful
bites, although they rarely attack a
human hand unless they mistake it
for food. Morays hunt by smell and

have poor eyesight. When feeding eels, it is always a good idea to use a set of long-handled tongs to avoid any nasty accidents.

Several species of moray eel are commonly available and while some make interesting and rewarding aquarium inhabitants, others are best left in the wild. Suitable species for a medium-sized aquarium include the snowflake moray *(Echnida nebulosa)*, which has speckled coloration that blends well into rocky crevices. The snowflake is relatively small for an eel, rarely exceeding 60cm (24in) in captivity, and will usually accept frozen lancefish and shrimps. For the larger aquarium, the reticulated moray *(Gymnothorax tesselatus)* is relatively undemanding. It can quickly grow to about 1m (39in) and is extremely powerful, so make sure that all rockwork is firmly glued into place before purchasing one of these fish. Morays are generally not suited to invertebrate aquariums, as they have a tendency to knock over corals as they slide around the tank in search of food.

When keeping morays, it is imperative to use a tight-fitting, robust aquarium lid, as these fish are expert escape artists. Morays can escape through seemingly impossible small gaps and a favourite avenue for escape is the cut-out areas of cover glasses in the corners of an aquarium. Always block up these corners to prevent unexpected losses!

One species not recommended for the aquarium is the ribbon eel *(Rhinomuraenia amboinensis)*. These fish are seen either as a blue or black variant and, although highly attractive, they do not adapt well to captive life. Many ribbon eels starve to death, and their availability to the hobbyist cannot really be justified.

Opistognathidae – jawfishes

The main appeal of the often subtly coloured jawfishes is their highly entertaining behaviour. They never stray far from their burrows or shells and usually hover directly above their escape route on the constant lookout for danger. Jawfishes tend to pounce out of their homes to grab at a passing meal and are amazingly quick to retreat, tail first, back into their hole when they have caught their food. At night, they often close

Right: Jawfishes (Opistognathus aurifrons) *require a deep, soft substrate so that they can dig themselves a home.*

119

the entrance to their accommodation with a small pebble or shell.

Jawfishes can be kept in a group, providing sufficient bolt-holes are available. They are easy to maintain and an excellent addition to any reef aquarium. In tanks with large, more boisterous species, these small, peaceful fish can become intimidated, so they are best suited to aquariums housing small, non-aggressive fish.

Ostraciontidae – boxfishes and cowfishes

Boxfishes and cowfishes are highly distinctive in shape and behaviour and are some of the 'characters' of the aquarium world. With their bony, boxlike shape and seemingly under-developed fins, they are not suited to fast swimming and do not appreciate aquariums with a powerful water flow. In a small, peaceful aquarium setup they will live happily with other species of a similar disposition.

Boxfishes and cowfishes are quite demanding species to keep. Being slow swimmers, they are a target for many more aggressive fish, and they are susceptible to bacterial diseases. In addition, as a deterrent to potential predators, these fish can release a poison into the water when threatened. This can have disastrous consequences in an aquarium, wiping out all the livestock in extreme cases. If you select either of these species, ask to see them feeding before making a purchase and make sure they are well fed. They can be difficult to feed in captivity and will quickly starve if the right food cannot be found. Due to their behaviour when threatened and their lack of swimming ability, these species are suited to quiet aquariums, where they will feel safe. Although generally suitable for reef tanks, they do tend to pick at the heads of tubeworms and soft corals.

Below: Surely one of the most bizarre marine species! The long-horned cowfish (Lactoria cornuta) is truly well-named.

Platacidae – batfish

With their laterally compressed bodies and high fins, the very distinctive batfish resemble freshwater angelfish. In the wild, they are often found among mangrove tree roots, where they blend in well with the leaves and roots of the tree.

Two species are commonly available: the round batfish *(Platax orbicularis)* and the more colourful

Above: It is not difficult to see why the stunning red-faced batfish (Platax pinnatus) would attract the marine fishkeeper. However, it is a difficult species to keep in the aquarium, and the red coloration fades in adulthood.

red-faced batfish *(P. pinnatus)*. *P. orbicularis* usually adapts well to aquarium life, growing to about 40cm (16in) and accepting a wide

Above: In their juvenile stage, these adult emperor angelfish (Pomacanthus imperator) *have completely different coloration. Young fish have white bars on a multitoned blue background.*

Below: Flame angelfish (Centropyge loriculus) *are among the most vivid marine species and highly sought after for reef aquariums. Provide a diet that includes plenty of greenstuff.*

variety of foods. However, *Platax pinnatus* is not as easy to maintain in an aquarium and is recommended only for the most experienced hobbyist. It requires optimum water conditions and will not tolerate anything but the lowest nitrate levels. In addition, it is often reluctant to feed in captivity, so if you are thinking of keeping a red-faced batfish, insist on seeing it feeding in the shop before you buy.

Batfish require aquariums at least 60cm (24in) deep and will grow quickly. They are peaceful fish and often the victims of fin-nipping, so keep them only with other non-aggressive species. Although attractive as juveniles, they do lose their colour and become more rounded with age, often completely losing their angelfish appearance.

Pomacanthidae – angelfish

Angelfishes vary greatly in shape and colour between species and are highly sought-after for their often striking colour patterns. In this book, we have separated the family into large species and the *Centropyge* genus of dwarf angelfishes.

Large angelfish are generally unsuited to invertebrate aquariums, as many tend to pick at coral heads and tubeworms. While generally omnivorous, some species have dietary requirements that make them unsuitable for the majority of aquariums. For example, the regal angel *(Pygoplites diacanthus)* grazes on sponges in the wild and in many cases does not readily adapt to aquarium foods. However, most large angels will accept a variety of foods and benefit greatly from the inclusion of greens such as spinach and lettuce to replace their natural diet of algae.

Part of the appeal of angelfishes is the dramatic colour change they often undergo during their transformation from juvenile to adult. Adult species of this family, such as the emperor angelfish *(Pomacanthus imperator)*, the French *(P. paru)* and the blue ring *(P. annularis)*, are totally different from their juvenile colour forms and do not adapt as quickly as juveniles to captive life. When buying, choose strong juvenile specimens that are feeding boldly and not overly skittish.

Angelfish are not generally suited to the beginner, as they are susceptible to disease when kept in less than ideal water conditions. They require large aquariums and, while generally peaceful, are usually intolerant of their own species.

Dwarf angelfish, such as the cherub *(Centropyge argi)*, the fireball *(C. acanthops)* and the flame *(C. loriculus)*, are extremely popular aquarium inhabitants. They rarely exceed 9cm (3.5in) and are usually peaceful, 'invertebrate-friendly' fish, although they can be intolerant of their own species.

Dwarf angelfish require a variety of foods, including green food, and extensive rockwork in which to hide if nervous. These delightful fish are well suited to most aquariums but, as with their larger relatives, must have good water conditions to thrive. High nitrate levels may lead to a rapid deterioration in health.

Pomacentridae – damselfishes and clownfishes

This family contains probably the two most common and easily recognizable groups of fishes: damselfish and clown, or anemone, fish. Damsels, including the ever-popular green chromis *(Chromis caerulea)* and electric-blue damsel *(Pomacentrus coeruleus)*, are available in every retail outlet selling marine livestock. Although there are many species of damsel, the majority are a variety of shades of blue, with other colours sometimes thrown in.

These small shoaling fish are relatively hardy and often the first aquarium inhabitants chosen by marine hobbyists. Their reputation as a tough, tolerant species often means that they are offered up as sacrificial filtration starters – a totally unacceptable practice. Damsels are as susceptible to disease as other fish, and although they tolerate slightly higher nitrate and nitrite levels in the short term, this is no excuse for poor aquarium water quality.

Damsels can be housed singly, but tend to show less aggression towards other fish when kept in groups of five or more. They are easy to feed and adapt well to aquariums of any size. They are ideal inhabitants for invertebrate aquariums.

Clownfishes are the archetypal marine fish. They are well known for their symbiotic relationship with anemones, which accounts for their alternative common name of anemonefish. These pretty fish are usually orange, with a variety of white and yellow stripes, depending

Below: Tomato clownfishes (Amphiprion ephippium), *or fire clowns as they are also known, can be aggressive and are best kept singly. They are ideal inhabitants for invertebrate aquariums.*

Left: Percula clowns (Amphiprion percula) *are everybody's idea of a marine fish! They are happiest living amongst the tentacles of a sea anemone, where they are prevented from being stung by the mucus coating on their skin.*

Below: Abudefduf saxatilis *(the sergeant major) is one of many species of damselfish commonly available. This family of fish is generally hardy and makes an ideal choice for the beginner.*

Above: False grammas (Pseudochromis paccagnellae) *are naturally shy, but will gain confidence if provided with sufficient rockwork in which to hide. They feed readily on a variety of foods.*

on the species. Being poor swimmers, they 'waddle' in the water, rather than swim. Clowns rarely stray far from the security of the reef and can usually be found in a host anemone, where their mucus layer protects them from the anemone's stinging tentacles. It is thought that their host benefits from the food they drop.

Clownfish have regularly been bred in aquariums, and are increasingly being supplied to shops from commercial captive breeding programmes (see page 50). They will accept most foods and are ideal inhabitants for invertebrate aquariums. Although generally

peaceful, beware of the extremely aggressive maroon clown *(Premnas biaculeatus)* and the sometimes territorial tomato clown *(Amphiprion ephippium).*

Pseudochromidae – pygmy basslets

Pygmy basslets generally share the same characteristics and requirements as fish from the family Grammidae. Like the grammas, they are usually extremely shy at first, but can become less reclusive given time. They require plenty of hiding places and are ideal choices for invertebrate aquariums, although they may fight with their own and similar species. Particularly popular choices include the flash back *(Pseudochromis diadema)*, the false gramma *(Pseudochromis paccagnellae)* and the strawberry gramma

(Pseudochromis porphyreus), each with its own distinctive, bright coloration. The false gramma is often incorrectly labelled in shops as a royal gramma, but can be distinguished from the latter by the more distinct break in coloration between the magenta front and the yellow back half of the body.

Below: The lionfish (Dendrochirus zebra) *is an ambush hunter, capable of engulfing fish up to one-third its own size. It also has a powerful stinging toxin in the spines on the dorsal fin rays.*

Scorpaenidae – lionfishes

The highly unusual shape and patterning of this family of fish is unmistakable. Lionfish are commonly offered for sale and can make excellent aquarium fish if kept correctly. They are renowned predators, engulfing their prey whole, and anything capable of fitting into their large jaws is likely to disappear from the aquarium. Lionfish either ambush their would-be meals by hiding amongst corals and reef rock, or they sidle up to their prey before lunging at it. However, their appetite

is not the only reason for their notoriety, as their decorative dorsal spines are highly poisonous, so treat these fish with respect. Their sting is extremely nasty and hospital care may be required if you are stung.

These fish are peaceful among fish too large to eat, and may be kept with corals, but not with shrimps, which form part of their natural diet. When buying a lionfish, always ensure that the specimen will accept dead foods, such as lancefish and whole shrimp, mussels, etc. Do not feed lionfish with other live fish. Apart from the ethical issues, there is always a chance that the lionfish could become diseased if fed with another live fish.

Serranidae – wreckfishes and groupers

The grouper side of this family is an extremely popular one for larger aquariums. The fish have large mouths and will consume any small fish that happens to swim past. Keep them only with fish too large to eat.

Particularly popular and easy to maintain are the panther grouper (Chromileptis altivelis), with its highly distinctive polkadot patterning, and the marine betta (Calloplesiops altivelis), which uses its false eyespot to deceive potential prey into thinking that it is facing away from them.

Many groupers can grow very large and very quickly, so they need suitably sized aquariums. However, the marine betta, with a maximum size of about 15cm (6in), is suited to medium-sized tanks.

Above: Lyretail coralfish (Pseudanthias squamipinnis) *are found in huge shoals on reefs around the world. The fishes' orange-pink coloration appears far darker in deep water, rendering them less visible in the wild than in the aquarium.*

Most groupers can be housed with sessile (sedentary) invertebrates, although they should not be kept with crustaceans, as these may prove too tempting a meal for them!

Wreckfish are far more suited to invertebrate tanks, and one species in particular, the lyretail coralfish

(Pseudanthias squamipinnis), is
extremely popular. In the wild, these
fish are seen swimming in large
shoals, just off the reef face.
Wreckfish are bright orange, with the
males displaying an extended third
dorsal ray and even brighter colours
than their female counterparts. These
fish are best kept in groups of five or
more, where they will often display
their natural tendency to shoal.
Wreckfish are bold fish that will
accept a wide variety of meaty foods,
as well as relishing an occasional live
food treat, such as brineshrimp.

Siganidae – rabbitfishes

Rabbitfishes are laterally compressed
and distinctly oblong in shape. In this
small family, rabbitfishes are more
often than not represented in the
aquarium world by only one species,
the foxface *(Lo vulpinus)*. It is a
bright yellow colour, with very
distinctive face markings, which
account for its other common name
of badgerfish. This species adapts
well to aquarium life and will accept
a wide variety of foods, but make
sure that plenty of green foods are
always available, as the foxface is a

Above: *The foxface, or badgerfish, (Lo vulpinis) gets its name from its facial markings. Juveniles are more vividly marked than adults. From a young age, these fish have a poisonous dorsal and anal spine that can cause a painful injury.*

constant algae grazer. When stressed or if it is disturbed at night, the foxface takes on a blotchy grey appearance. There is one important point to note when keeping these fish: the dorsal and anal spines are poisonous and can inflict a nasty sting. When threatened, the dorsal spines are often raised up from their usually flat appearance.

Rabbitfish should be kept in large, fish-only aquariums and have plenty of swimming space, as well as a refuge at night.

Syngnathidae – seahorses and pipefish

Seahorses are an instantly recognizable and extremely popular species that, if kept properly, can be easy to maintain and immensely rewarding. These shy fish are highly distinctive in shape and have a fascinating method of reproduction that adds to their appeal. For the few weeks before they hatch, the male seahorse incubates the eggs in a pouch. After about five weeks, the male 'gives birth' to tiny, perfectly formed seahorses. This species is

Right: *Despite their popularity – due both to their unique appearance and behaviour – seahorses are not suited to beginners. They have specific dietary requirements, especially when young.*

quite easy to breed and maintain, although a lack of understanding of their requirements on the part of too many hobbyists leads to many seahorses dying a premature death. Today, there is plenty of information available on this species and anyone hoping to keep seahorses is strongly urged to research the subject first.

However, in brief, seahorses require an aquarium devoid of boisterous fish, with plenty of anchor points around which they can curl their tails. In the wild, they attach themselves to corals, such as gorgonians, and snatch at food as it drifts past them in the current. Seahorses are poor swimmers, and require plenty of live foods, such as mysis and brineshrimp, in order to

Above: Pipefish are suited to species aquariums or quiet reef tanks. Feed them regularly with live and frozen foods. This is the bluestripe (Doryrhamphus excisus).

flourish. As with any marine fish, make sure that they are feeding before buying them. Fortunately, many seahorses offered for sale today are captive-bred; in fact, there are several worldwide programmes to reintroduce captive-bred species back into the wild in order to bolster naturally dwindling populations.

Pipefish are extremely delicate fish that require similar conditions to those preferred by seahorses. They need very regular feeding with live foods and are extremely shy. Once again, commercial breeding of species such as the bluestripe pipefish *(Doryrhamphus excisus)* has made keeping these interesting fish considerably easier.

Tetraodontidae – pufferfishes

Puffers are easy to maintain in fish-only systems, but must be kept away from invertebrates at all costs due to their penchant for crunching corals. Their fused jaw is extremely strong, and these fish benefit from a diet of shellfish, such as whole cockle, and other meaty foods.

Puffers can inflate themselves when threatened, so handle them with care when making a purchase.

It is a good idea to ask the retailer to place them into a dark bag for transportation in order to reduce stress. Despite their outwardly fierce appearance, these fish are generally slow-swimming and peaceful and will often quickly become tame. However, you should exercise some caution, as their skin is poisonous, and when stressed they can excrete a toxin into the water.

Below: Valentini puffers (Canthigaster valentini) *are relatively easy to maintain, but are not to be trusted with invertebrates. Their beaklike mouth houses strong teeth for crushing corals.*

INDEX

CREDITS

The publishers would like to thank the following photographers for providing images, credited here by page number and position: B(Bottom), T(Top), C(Centre), BL(Bottom left), etc.

David Allison: 67(BL), 107
ARDEA (London): 8(Kurt Amsler)
M P & C Piednoir/Aqua Press: 33, 38, 45, 56, 68, 72, 80, 94-95, 97(T),
98-99, 105, 119, 120, 134
Bruce Coleman Collection: 16(Franco Banfi), 54(Jen & Des Bartlett),
87(Franco Banfi), 108(B, Jane Burton)
Peter Burgess: 35(T)
Les Holliday: 26, 35(B), 42, 47, 50-51, 59
Natural Visions: 12(Richard Coomber), 15(Soames Summerhayes), 28(Jeff Collett),
44(Soames Summerhayes) 57(Soames Summerhayes), 69(Jeff Collett)
Arend van den Nieuwenhuizen: 32, 106, 108(T), 112
Kim Osborn: 27, 77
Photomax (Max Gibbs): Half-title page, Title page, 10, 22, 29, 30, 46, 48, 92-93, 96, 100,
101(T,B), 102-103, 104, 110(T,B), 111(T,B), 113, 114, 115(T,B), 116, 117, 118, 121, 122(T,B),
124-125, 126, 127, 128-129, 130, 131, 132, 133
Mike Sandford: 23

The practical photographs have been taken by Geoffrey Rogers and are © Interpet Publishing.
The artwork illustrations have been prepared by Phil Holmes and
Stuart Watkinson and are © Interpet Publishing.

ACKNOWLEDGMENTS

The publishers would like to thank the following for their help during the preparation of this book: Dr Peter Burgess; Carl Gericke; Julian Hastings, Arcadia; Heaver Tropics, Ash, Kent; Phil Jones, San Francisco Bay Brand; Rosslab plc, Gravesend, Kent; Dr Steve La Thangue.